MW00588531

Choose Your Friends,

Choose Your Life

Confessions of a married man

By the same author

My Love Affair With Italy

Choose Your Friends, Choose Your Life

Anna,

One of the brightest
Cousins I have.

Love You

Preston

Cousin Anna,

Thank you for being a
part of our special day—
Love,
Khakie

Choose Your Friends, Choose Your Life

Confessions of a married man

Preston Young & Debbie Mancuso

Preston Young & Debbie Mancuso

Copyright © 2021 by Deborah A. Mancuso

All rights reserved.

No part of this book may be reproduced in any written, electronic, recording, or photocopying without written permission of the publisher or author. The exception would be in the case of brief quotations embodied in the critical articles or reviews and pages where permission is specifically granted by the author, Debbie Mancuso.

Although every precaution has been taken to verify the accuracy of the information contained herein, the author and publisher assume no responsibility for any errors or omissions. No liability is assumed for damages that may result from the use of information contained within.

Published by: A Passion for Italy, Lyndhurst, NJ
www.Facebook.com/MyLoveAffairWithItaly

Creative Consultant: Rita Chraim

Books may be purchased by contacting the publisher and author at: dmancuso310@gmail.com

ISBN: 978-0-9989732-4-1

10 9 8 7 6 5 4 3 2 1

1. Memoir

First Edition

Printed in the United States of America

I dedicate this book to my kids and grandkids who still call to tell me they love me, and to my wife who kept the porch light burning for over six years.

"Life is partly what we make it, and partly what it is made by the friends we choose."
– Tennessee Williams

Preston Young & Debbie Mancuso

Preface

Preston's life journey began in a comfortable, traditional Jewish home in the 1940's on Long Island, New York. Preston is a smart and happy child, one of four young brothers growing up in an idyllic home, until at the age of 10 his family suffers the sudden, traumatic loss of his father, causing his family to unravel and move in entirely different directions. Preston is left with bitterness and resentment, the residual effects remaining with him throughout his life and causing him to make a series of bad decisions starting with the friends he chooses. A Dean Martin look-alike coming of age in the 1950s, his exceptionally good looks open many doors, many hearts, and many issues.

Choose Your Friends, Choose Your Life tells the story of how troubled kids were dealt with nearly three-quarters of a century ago and the resulting problems the "experts" created. This book describes the archaic ways of dealing with problem children who nearly all become problem adults, a How-NOT-To for anyone dealing with a child's devastation. *Choose Your Friends, Choose Your Life* gives personal, honest portrayals and insights of both mens' and womens' sexuality spanning six decades, even describing how men procured women.

Eventually Preston's bad deeds caught up with him, and it takes a woman from his past to draw him back into life.

ACKNOWLEDGEMENTS

The authors wish to acknowledge Gina Wangrycht for taking on the job of editing, and to Rita Chraim for her help and support on the covers.

Preston Young & Debbie Mancuso

Introduction

As a proper southerner there are austere rules and social graces when meeting someone- keep it short and sweet, no religion, no politics, no unsavory topics. I broke all those rules.

Several years' back when blessed with the good fortune of old friends, my husband and I found ourselves tucked in a family vineyard in Tuscany with a handful of other guests. It would be our respite from the changing world, even if for a brief moment. Italy is a place that doesn't change not because the people are incapable; it's because they know they have something here that never needs changing. Something about the place brings out the best in us. With storied wineries meandering through steep switchbacks and meticulous, cultivated vines, the pace is slower and largely unspoiled in Tuscany. There is never a sense of urgency here. With time for once on my side, I introduced myself one evening to a gentleman after passing his open window. I abhor small talk and the effort often associated with it. I don't need to talk about myself, and I don't need to be pulled into other's issues. (You know those times when you engage with a stranger and wish you could rewind time and go back even a minute.) Yet, I still adhered to my southern upbring hoping I didn't regret that decision to introduce myself. A few pleasantries were exchanged, and I sincerely extended an offer to join us on the communal patio. I went on my way never expecting anything more.

Later I noticed that nice looking gentlemen donning a beret approaching our table. Without hesitation and before proper introductions, we poured him a glass after he was subjected to a seedy question about some discussion we were engaged in. My southern manners had disappeared. Was it the flow of the wine, the sense of place or the ease the gentlemen eluded? Without batting an eye, he answered and quickly returned the favor. We dealt him into our card game. The wine disappeared and I couldn't tell you who won. That never matters. Hours faded just as any pretenses we might have brought. The elixir of the vines and the heavy-handed pours probably played a role in our friendly banter, but perhaps it was the connection with people that occurs when nothing is expected or wanted. In Preston I found a kindred soul, someone I knew had an interesting story. Everyone has a story, some are just told better than others, some are peppered with cringe worthy events, some sown with mountains of sadness and some stories are still being written.

An odd band of misfits circled that table during those nights of cards and dinner. As fog rolled in casting a cool chill, a strong and immediate connection could be felt. It was beyond quiet, the backdrop of solitude, blissfully removed from pressing problems or current issues. Although never eerie, the quietness of the unspoiled backdrop of rolling hills running throughout could be heaven or hell depending on your outlook. Preston showed the beauty that was before us. He wasn't bitter about lost time, family or decisions good and bad. He put that behind him. Old enough to be my father, Preston was not running to or from something, but relishing the present. Absorbing the sun-dappled vistas I realized I was on autopilot in my world often missing things standing right in front of me. Preston was in front of me. He wasn't living in the past; he was present and not looking beyond. We came together with openness of mind, but never emptiness both lacking today in most people. Perhaps his life circumstances vastly varied from mine and an unusual pairing, but we all really want the same things: family, friends, and faith. Maybe it's a different order for each of us, but it's how we get these things in our own order that makes our life whole. Preston has had a lifetime to figure and arrange his order and his story is still being written. Nothing is off limits with Preston. No question taboo. We both possess strong and differing religious backgrounds, sometimes similar political views, opposing views in musical taste, and a strong affinity for questionable jokes. On paper we don't match. But that's paper failing to consider real human connection. We both share a curiosity about this world and most importantly we respect each other and the differences associated with that. It was the time that turned a dream escape into a collision of fate that unfolded, a part of the natural architect of our story.

My husband and I bid our farewells to Preston unsure if we would see each other again. We walked the short distance to our villa with a sense of fullness; we both agreed it was a fitting end to a magical time. My story with Preston didn't end, but rather was just beginning.

I reflect on what was it that Preston offered. Perhaps it was the wine or the (legal) narcotic effect of the shared meals, but really I know it was the lack of pretenses he brought. Just like the vines that incased that mythical place sometimes producing less than desirable results and requiring pruning, life is like that. We adjust to the place and trim the people and things in our lives that offer little. Preston is a testament to adjusting to his place and pruning the people who hinder shaping a beautiful life. I believe it is his resilience that gauges his life, not the decisions that he made.

I may have broken proper southern rules and social graces, but I learned to bend and change my stance on small talk somewhat because it's all those unscripted moments that seem to stay with us long after the adventure is done. This is one of those experiences that moved from a holiday escape to a story that is still being written.

I recommend you approach Preston's story with the openness and earnestness that he was willing to share. Enjoy.

-Christine

Contents

Preston Young & Debbie Mancuso

Chapter One

The Nightmare Ends

lready 72 years of age, my body was tired, exhausted from years of abuse and stress, but my head and my heart were racing that night like that of a young boy going on his first date who was contemplating all the possibilities. But it was far more serious than any first date. I had been waiting for that day for nearly a decade.

That night would be the very last one I would share a room with 69 other men and be subjected to the overwhelming stench that pervaded the entire floor. Like most of the nights, it was somewhat silent in the early hours of the morning, except for when a few guys would leave their radios turned on to conceal their vibrant whispers. The extra sounds were never appreciated, and most of the time they'd be angrily instructed to shut them off by the other inmates or a guard unless the inmate listening to the radio was rather large, in which case, he'd be left alone. Then

1

morning would come, and I'd meet each day with little enthusiasm.

For those last ten years, I'd gone to bed each night and repeatedly asked myself the same thing every time my head hit the pillow: "How did I get here? How could this have happened," and, of course, the inevitable, "How did it ever go that far?" The conversation with myself always started the same: *One day I'm a 63-year-old respectable business owner living in a beautiful, middle-class suburb, and the next day my address is hell.* A precipitous fall, to say the least. And then I would remember how it happened, how it all happened. I told the truth. That's what I did! I told the truth. Whoever said "The truth will set you free" was a fucking liar — or they never had a wife. I got here telling the truth. That's exactly what I did!

As I tossed and turned all through the night, my excitement escalated with each passing minute knowing that the following morning my life would change dramatically. Unlike other events that transformed my life, like my first wedding or the frantic drives to the hospital waiting for my kids to be born, this change was going to release me from the

2

depths of hell. For the past eight years, my sole identity had been my federal identification number — digits ingrained in my brain. For every letter I wrote, every medical appointment I had, or every time I walked to an area where I was not immediately recognized, I was required to repeat my number. It was like being a foreigner in my own tiny country, and every time I moved to a different area, I needed to show my passport. Being of Jewish descent, I found this even more demeaning. I may not have been marked for the gas chambers, but I never knew if I was going to make it home alive.

That evening had been yet another cold, damp, bleak December night in New England, and as I stood at the window for the last time, I thought how different *that* night was — saying goodbye to 20 or so of the guys filled me with as much joy as a kid on Christmas Eve. My mind racing, I knew I was never going to be able to sleep. Peering out at the empty sky beyond the lot, I imagined how beautiful it was beyond the walls. I envisioned the homes lit with their Christmas lights that sparkled with the colors of the season, Santas and reindeers perched proudly atop the roofs, decorative

3

evergreen wreaths hanging on the doors, snowmen on the lawns built by the kids and their dads and, of course, the families decorating their freshly cut Christmas trees while listening to Bing Crosby singing "Silent Night." I even envied the people as they swiped their credit cards for their Christmas and Hanukkah gifts in the bustling stores, and the only thing that soothed my soul was knowing that I was going to be one of those people soon — or so I thought!

I had longed for the day when there would be no more bars, no more Bunkie's, no more mess hall food, and no more commissary, no more guards and wardens, and no more showering in groups. No more holding hands from across a table when I received a visitor, no more sleeping alone, and no more being treated like an animal. And never again would I have a humiliating cavity search or would I have to endure the insolence of a correctional officer. The following day I would become a free man — I would be a human again. I would also be getting another chance at life at the age of 72 and the long nightmare would be over.

When I first arrived here, I was certain it would only be a few years before I was able to resume my life again; however, I could not have been more wrong. As weeks turned into months and months into years, reality began to set in, and I knew nothing would ever be the same again. More and more I missed the things I had taken for granted my entire life before losing my freedom — the very things that make a person human. The long years I spent there had deprived me of the most fundamental of human needs: touch. And over time, the depravation left me wondering if I'd even remember how to kiss or how to make love when I got out. I only knew I desperately needed to be touched, and I needed it often.

As the sun finally rose that morning, I awakened with great fervor and began counting the minutes before the first guard would come to escort me to my exit from hell. I didn't even take the chance of going to breakfast for fear of missing the call! Finally, at 9 a.m., a guard arrived to bring me to another building where they would verify who I was before walking me out and releasing me back into the world I so desperately missed. But once I arrived, the anxiety of the night and the sleep deprivation caused me to forget my federal identification number. I sat there in absolute disbelief. How could I not know? For nearly a decade I had recited this number that had been pierced into my brain, and all I needed to be released that morning was to repeat it verbally from memory — the only thing! He could have asked me to recite the lyrics of my favorite 200 songs and I would have known them, but my prison number completely escaped me. Squinting his eyes, the guard austerely, almost angrily, repeated, "WHAT IS YOUR FEDERAL ID NUMBER?" But still nothing left my mouth. With my heart pounding and my stomach writhing, I asked him what would happen if I couldn't remember it, and I was advised that until I did, I was never going to be released. Bewildered and anxious, I sat for 10 minutes before the blood flowed back into my brain, finally giving me the ability to recall my number: 1 7 5 2 6 1.

Walking that interminable, proverbial last mile was taking the whole experience in reverse. Each time I walked through a set of steel doors and heard the loud, screeching clang locking me "out," my emotions heightened more than the previous set of steel doors. But this time, I was walking toward the light. I was going home.

Chapter Two
Looking for Dad

I t was the end of summer in New York City, 1939. Regular television broadcasts had just begun in the United States, Lou Gehrig retired from Major League Baseball after being diagnosed with ALS, the Brooklyn Dodgers were still in Brooklyn, and the United States hosted the World's Fair in New York City, the nation's first capital, on the 150th anniversary of George Washington's inauguration. World War II began in Europe; four more failed assassination attempts were made on Hitler's life that year alone, one by merely eight minutes; and President Roosevelt initiated the Americas A-Bomb Program after speaking to the physicist Albert Einstein. The average cost of a new home was $3,800, the median annual wage was a whopping $1,730; gasoline went as high as 10 cents a gallon; a new car was running about $700; the average rent was $28 per month; and a loaf of bread was 8 cents. Four of the best movies ever made were released that year: *Gone with the Wind, The Wizard of Oz, Stagecoach, and Wuthering Heights.* While Frank Sinatra was recording his first major hit song, "All or Nothing at All," (the very song that would shoot him to the top), my mother went into labor and had her own best production that year: Me.

My parents were Sylvia and Edward Yankowitz — first generation Russian and Romanian Jews. As she already had two sons, Mom was, I might say, anticipating a girl and calling her Priscilla. But as luck would not have it, she gave birth to her third son and awarded me the name Preston instead. Shortly thereafter we moved from Coney Island to an apartment in the densely populated borough of the Bronx, and by the time I was 6 years old, my father relocated us one last time to the idyllic place of Long Beach, also called "The City By the Sea," on Long Island's South Shore, because I had developed asthma and nearly died from the treatment itself. For some reason, the ocean air helped my breathing to the extent I never had a serious problem with it again. Two years later, my mother gave birth to her fourth and final child, another son.

Growing up, my mother was a housekeeper, and my father, a house painter. Although Dad was forced to quit school in 5th grade and was sent out to work, he was smart and quickly learned enough from working with other tradesmen to become a licensed contractor. Not long after moving to Long Beach, he opened his own business building low-income housing and, in just a few short years, began a successful career building single-family homes.

My childhood was ideal. My parents adored each other and were always affectionate. When they'd sing together, I'd play their conductor. On Sundays, my grandparents, aunts, and uncles congregated at our home, ate, and sang harmony. The only memory I have of my parents fighting was when I was 7 years old. It was December 24, and although we may have been Jewish, we, too, celebrated Santa Claus and even hung lights on our home and decorated a Christmas tree in our living room like any respectful Gentile family. Mom herself was joyous about the holiday and told me I was getting something special from Santa that year. Unable to control this infectious excitement, she went as far as to tell me that Santa had already left my presents. I didn't ask how she knew (given nothing was displayed in our living room), nor did I question why he came early; I just assumed it had something to do with us being Jewish. Leaping at this propitious moment to get a sneak-peak, I asked Mom to show it to me, and that's when she made the colossal mistake of agreeing — and even went further by allowing me to put it on! Santa had left me two outfits: one cowboy and one Indian. Just as I had finished putting on the Indian outfit, Dad walked through the door. He became enraged and sent me to my bedroom so he could argue with my mother. The following Christmas, however, he made certain there would be no repeat of this gross breach and kept my gift hidden from both of us until that Christmas morning. Before I awakened, he painted the side of the basement staircase with the words "Preston's Garage," and under that staircase was a fire truck large enough for me to ride.

My father was my hero. Everything I did I did for him, for his approval. He was the one who checked my homework, and on occasion he would even take me out of school to work with him and be his little

11

helper. When I was 8 years old, my father had a business matter in Florida and decided he was taking me — just me. We took a train down, and while there he purchased a DeSoto Suburban (a mini limo with a luggage rack) to drive home. It was just the two of us for weeks. I loved every moment we shared together. He taught me nearly everything I knew at such a tender age, pushed me to study hard, and in 5th grade, I achieved his goal and was proudly on top of my class. Then, in October 1949, just after my 10th birthday, our lives changed forever when Dad was taken to the hospital with chest pains. He would never return home again.

My hero was gone, and the family made the decision to keep me away from attending his funeral services. They were afraid how I'd react, and part of me thinks it was for their own benefit — they just didn't want to see how I'd react knowing how attached we were to each other. I wasn't allowed to say good-bye to my protector, my best friend, and this sudden and horrific event would be the beginning of my downward spiral.

My mother became overwhelmed raising four sons on her own, ages 2, 10, 15, and 17. On his death bed, Dad made Mom promise she would never go with another man. He either couldn't stand the thought of her being with another man or he was rightfully afraid how another man would treat his kids. Either way, she never broke her promise to her dying day.

Shortly after his passing, Mom was able to secure a job at our local chamber of commerce. Feeling aggrieved over our monumental loss, I started cutting school and hanging out with a bad crowd. Almost immediately, my grades dropped precipitously. I was no longer on top of the class and I didn't care. All I thought about was my father, how I didn't say good-bye to my dad, and my young mind couldn't accept that he was gone forever. Having no sense of closure, I started to look for him everywhere I went. For years I looked at every face in the crowd, sometimes even walking up to a man to realize it was not my father. My heart and mind would never accept it.

One day, when I was 15 years old, my older friend Gingi saw a one-armed bandit on his soda route in someone's garage and decided he wanted to steal it.

13

He couldn't manage doing it alone, and I agreed to help. Together we were able to lift it into his brother's car and drive away. But as people do when they are proud of their accomplishments, he told others who repeated the story, and the police were notified who was responsible for the heist. When my mother arrived at the police station and was informed of what happened, she did something she had never done before: she cracked me hard across my face in front of everyone. I was humiliated. But even that didn't stop me from getting into trouble. After that incident, I duplicated my brother Arnie's car key, and two or three times a week I would go to the train station where he parked it for work and take it for the day. Because I was tall, I was never stopped. That went on for about a year until I made the gross misjudgment and loaned my brother's car to a friend who was also a minor. He assured me the car would be returned to the station before my brother returned, but he didn't keep his word. When Arnie arrived at the station and didn't find his car, he came home and confronted me. As it turned out, he had been getting suspicious of me when the gas tank and the parking spot seemed to have been different all too often. Infuriated, he

14

punched me in the face. The car was found at my friend's home.

That New Year's Eve, my friends and I broke into a concession stand under the boardwalk that was closed for the winter. It was never planned, but I made the decision to follow them. All I took was a pack of gum with my favorite Brooklyn Dodgers baseball cards, and the others stole candy and potato chips. Not exactly a windfall. We were all arrested a few months later and sent to Mineola jail in Long Island for three full weeks before my court date. Because there were too many of us in my group, one of us had to be put into a different cell block with the older kids, and I, being the tallest, was chosen. Unfortunately, the cell block I was assigned to had about nine teenage boys. The way it was set up was each boy had a private cell, and each cell block had nine cells. In the morning, the guard would announce he was coming in with coffee. The cells had small openings in the bars that had a small platform, and as the guard sped past each cell, you would put your arm through the opening with your coffee cup in hand, and the guard would very quickly pour the coffee into it. On my first day, I

15

missed it completely because I didn't know the protocol of needing to be ready at a moment's notice. (I was in the first cell and, therefore, the first one to get coffee.) On the second day, I put my arm through the opening, but didn't have my coffee cup ready. The guard just poured the steaming hot coffee on my hand and then laughed. By the third day, I got my coffee and never missed again.

Twice a day the cells were opened, and we congregated in the common area immediately in front of the cells where we were served lunch and dinner and were able to watch a small T.V. You could take your food into your own cell, but the cells were left open, so if someone wanted to come in for any reason, there was nothing stopping them. The boys here were at least 3 or 4 years older than me, and their source of entertainment was to harass the younger ones. One guy, much larger than me, who had befriended me on my first day, came into my cell and started fighting me. As large and intimating as he was, I fought back, and because I defended myself, none of the others ever instigated a fight with me. I may have been safe, but I was able to painfully witness another young boy taken against his will into a cell and raped. All of us heard his screams and cries until he was silenced into submission out of fear. No officer ever came in.

I was 15 years old on the day of my court appearance, and the judge suggested that I be sent to a reformatory school for troubled boys. Without my father, Mom couldn't handle me, and as difficult as the decision was, she agreed. On April 1, 1955, Mom took me by train to Hawthorne Center in New York City where Hawthorne's "OD," (Officer of the Day), Dennis O'Shea, picked me up and delivered me to Hawthorne Cedar Knolls School. All I had was one suitcase containing the mere essentials and a new pair of pajamas Mom had purchased for me. She was struggling with the decision she made to send me away and was trying to make the best of it. I'm sure she was thinking how this would never have happened had Dad been around.

After losing my father, my life changed dramatically overnight. It was blighted. One day I had everything, and the next day the loneliness and bitterness became palpable. I had been left back in school by now, and all my Jewish friends became estranged from me, leaving me with the bad kids to befriend. My mom began working full time, and there were so many years between my brothers and me that we were never close. Feeling lost already, I was leaving nothing behind and possessed a positive attitude of what was to come at the reformatory school. I viewed it as a new adventure I would be taking for the next 2 ½ years.

I entered Hawthorne Cedar Knolls School run by the Jewish Board of Guardians. All the residents there were either victims of abuse, had suffered severe neglect, or had lost family members and friends – often due to horrific circumstances. The grounds covered approximately 20 acres of land with 11 two-story buildings called "cottages." Seven cottages housed the boys on the left side of the grounds as you entered, and four for the girls on the right. The first floor of each cottage consisted of a T.V. room and the "parents'" apartment, and the second floor contained all the bedrooms, 3 to 4 kids in a room. In total, there were about 25 kids to each cottage, and each cottage had only one set of "parents" and one night watchman! There was no physical barrier dividing the boys from the girls' cottages, but it was strictly forbidden to cross over. Like a prison, you could be put into the "hole" had you been discovered on the other side.

When we arrived late in the afternoon, the OD dropped me off in my assigned cottage, number 19, where all the boys were between the ages of 15 and 18 years old. There, I briefly met my new "parents" who showed me to my room. It was nothing like the excitement you might expect between an orphaned child and his new adoptive parents, though. I was just another troubled kid they had to deal with — one of 25 difficult boys! It was dinnertime, so I left my belongings and was told to head to the dining hall. The dining hall was in a separate building and was divided by seven alcoves. Each alcove had long wooden tables and was assigned to one cottage. You could probably imagine how loud it got when there were 75 "damaged" teenage boys eating, talking, and fighting! Fortunately, some of the kids were friendly and struck up a normal conversation with me. But that wouldn't last long.

After dinner, I was told to head to the gym with the rest of the boys to play basketball, and I walked

19

with them. Now, I was always a good basketball player, and when the ball was bouncing in my direction, I took it and made the shot. The problem was one of the kids from my cottage, Donnie Weinstein, was going after the ball and expected me to throw it to him, but I wanted to show off my abilities and prove how I fit in. That wasn't acceptable to them. I was the new kid and they needed to show me who was running the place. He was pissed and tried throwing the ball to hurt me but missed. On the way back to the cottage, no one walked with me. The weaker kids knew better than to befriend me. When I retired to my bedroom, none of my roommates were there, so I got into my new pajamas. Now, I was from the suburbs, not a tough neighborhood to say the least, even though I managed to find other kids to get into trouble with. I dressed like I was from the 'burbs, but most of these kids were from the city and wouldn't think of wearing my matching nightwear. They were too cool for that. First, one kid walked into my room making fun of them and proceeded to start swinging at me over the basketball issue, making the point who was boss. But I wasn't afraid to swing back. He wasn't getting anywhere, and then five other boys came in to beat the shit out of me. They covered my head with the blanket and continued to punch and kick me. I found out quickly that the bullies ran the house and not the so-called "parents." As it turned out, the only positive feature in the cottage was the piano we were allowed to play. It was there where I was able to learn enough from playing around on the keyboard that I was able to perform for others.

We didn't attend a normal school because nearly all of us were considered flight risks. Instead, we attended school in the administrative building on the grounds. My classes consisted of English, math, and woodshop. For some reason, I was eventually allowed off the premises and attended a printing school where a bunch of us were driven and picked up. It was very much like a prison in every aspect; we had essentially no freedom, weren't allowed to mingle with the girls, and the teachers and all the other authorities freely hit us. One day after an instructor got upset with me, he lashed out and yelled, "You think this place is bad; you're probably going to wind up in a real prison one day like Valhalla." This federal prison was merely a few miles away. Little did I ever imagine how true these words would become.

The school's regulations dictated you could not have visitors for the first six months — not even your mother. They wanted the kids to become acclimated, or maybe it was so they'd have free range to screw us up even more. How was this helping any troubled kid? Even inmates are allowed visitors. What psycho decided that beating a kid and treating him like a prisoner would make him behave? So, not only were we subjected to beatings from the other kids, but those in charge could abuse us as well. Not the kind of adventure I had hoped for.

Six months after my arrival, we received a new set of "parents," which should have been called "grandparents" in our cottage, as they were a husband and wife in their late 50s. He was a goofy looking guy, overweight and always sweating. His wife was timid and rarely spoke to us. When we'd see her in the evening as we walked through the house, she was always smiling, but there was never any interaction. Not exactly like a real parent. The people who took these jobs were typically down on their luck themselves and were desperate. They had no background or education in psychology or any other science. No skills required, yet they were giving the job of parenting all these troubled kids to nearly anyone. They were essentially babysitters watching to make sure no one burned down the building. If the husband wanted to talk to me, he'd come up to our room a half hour after lights out and after he had a few drinks and ask if we were involved in one thing or another. He'd slur his words shamelessly and when he left ambling down the stairs, we'd hear him talk to himself and we'd all laugh. They were our "parents" for about a year until he was fired for drinking.

It had been five years since my dad passed, and my mom's best friend convinced her to go to a dance. She reluctantly agreed and decided to purchase new high-heeled shoes for the occasion. But merely days before the big night out, Mom was walking on the sidewalk and collapsed. She was diagnosed with multiple sclerosis and would never walk again. When she arrived to visit me that very first time six months later, she was in a wheelchair. She told me not to be embarrassed of her in a chair, and I told her that I wasn't, but the trust was that I was.

After a year or so of arriving at Hawthorne, I was allowed to go to my Aunt Mae and Uncle Irving's home in the Bronx for the weekend where my youngest brother Robert, who was 8 at the time, was living. My mother was living in the Helen Hayes Rehab Center in Rockland County, my oldest brother Arnie was living alone in our family home, and Norman had entered the Air Force. My visits to my aunt and uncle's home were allowed every 3 to 4 months during my second year at Hawthorne, and as time went on, I was allowed weekend visits more often. But soon thereafter, I could no longer take living under these conditions and planned to run away.

I didn't know where I was going, but I was leaving Hawthorne. When any one of us was planning to go AWOL, the other kids gave him a few dollars to help the effort. I was no exception. On that day, I ran through the woods, down the hill, and hid in the bushes by the train station until the train approached and paid when I was onboard. Unfortunately, one of the officers from the home was on the train and saw me, and the escape was foiled. A second attempt was made a few months later, and I was able to make my way to Manhattan. The first night I slept in Central Park on a hard park bench, and the second night I stayed in a sleezy motel that offered hourly rates. I had enough money for six hours. After two days, I ran out of cash and called Hawthorne. I was instructed to go to the Jewish Board of Guardians on 57th Street in Manhattan where someone from the home would pick me up.

About a year later, I made my final break. I made it to Manhattan again where I knew of an employment office on Warren Street. I was lucky enough to get a job as a pot washer all the way in Brooklyn where I was provided a room in the same building. But after three weeks, I could no longer take that either and phoned Hawthorne's principal of education, Mr. Krohn, who also lived on the school grounds, and told him exactly what I was doing and that I wanted to return to Hawthorne. Of all the adult superiors, he was the most compassionate. Without a word or expression of condescension, he benevolently agreed. I plaintively requested that if I did return, I

25

wouldn't be punished and went further to say that I wanted to attend the Christmas party. He agreed. Until the day I turned 18 and left Hawthorne for good, I never got into any more trouble. He kept his word, and I kept mine.

After the second year, I heard about a kid in cottage 9, Mike Middleman, who also liked to sing. Together with another kid, Warren Geller, we started a trio, a version of street corner singers, and sang throughout the grounds. Hawthorne put on plays every three months or so, and we performed for nearly all of them. Singing was my favorite pastime and probably the one thing that kept me from insanity. Not only did I enjoy singing, but it brought me back to days when my parents, aunts, and uncles would get together and harmonize, but mostly, it made me feel closer to my dad.

That year I also started playing football there. The tryouts were extremely rigorous, and several boys were hurt just trying to make the team. They separated the boys into two groups: the boys who were already on the team and dressed in full uniform with helmets and the new guys who had the leftover gear, typically no shoulder pads or helmets. The seasoned players were instructed to charge head-on with the ball to be tackled by the boy trying out for the team. Many of the kids were either hurt or were so frightened by the athletic prowess of the boys coming after them that they never even tried to tackle their opponents and, therefore, were swiftly eliminated. But I knew how to tackle without getting hurt by using a cross-body block and made the team. Coach Smithline was a tough guy, a former Marine, and took no crap from anyone. I worked hard to gain his respect the first year with no apparent success. But by the second year, I played well enough to become his quarterback, still receiving no recognition. It was our last game, and I knew how much this game meant to him since we did not have a real winning season. It came down to the very last play, and we were behind one touchdown. I stood tall, extended my arm, and threw the ball as hard as I could into the end zone and amazingly was caught by one of our guys for the winning touchdown. I immediately looked at Smithline standing across the field, and when our eyes met, he put his fingers together, kissed them, and made the motion of throwing the kiss to me. That moment would end up being the best day I ever had at

27

Hawthorne; it was the one and only time I was ever shown any respect or appreciation. That kiss would remain with me my entire life.

One of the few times the girls were allowed to sit near us was during football games. That was where I met Cookie. Like me, she was Jewish. A petite blonde, she was sexy and wasn't afraid to flirt — big time. I was not an experienced lover, to say the least, but I wasn't afraid to speak to girls and had my first kiss as far back as grammar school. But Cookie was far more advanced. Most of the girls I met at Hawthorne were. Maybe that is why they were sent there — their parents couldn't control them. Other than these games or our annual New Year's Eve dance, we were not allowed to see each other, nor were we allowed to even communicate. There were boys who had jobs like a plumber's helper that came in contact with the girls, so we would give that kid a note to pass to a certain girl. We would write and let them know when we would be passing by a specific spot just to get to wave to each other or say a few words. That was all. But, on occasion, we would meet up in the middle of the night to be alone for a while. Cookie and I did that for six months. Then one day I received a "Dear John" note from her. For the next 24 hours, I couldn't stop crying. I didn't cry because Cookie was breaking up with me, it was everything: my environment, my mom's condition, no longer having my Long Beach friends, no longer being in a regular school and being treated like a normal kid, but mostly it was the absence of my dad. It took five years to really hit me — five years of looking for him in the crowds — and when it did hit me, it was a tsunami of emotions. Everywhere I went, I sobbed. I would lay in a field and sob. I'd go to my cottage and I'd sob. The tears wouldn't stop. No one came near me that day — no one.

One day, a Columbia University psychologist who was given a grant to study us, moved into our cottage. Professor Howard Polsky was a very tall, heavyset man, and had a strange sounding voice, almost like from another planet. We nicknamed him "Animal." Animal gathered us into groups and advised he was doing a study on us and would be living in our cottage for six months. He said he would be asking us questions as he went along but we weren't required to answer if we weren't comfortable.

29

We were assured he wanted to be one of us. One afternoon, not long after Animal arrived, he walked over to the playground area where a few of us were playing basketball and asked to be included. He wasn't so quick with the ball, but he did have some moves and immediately started to gain respect.

A few months later, a bunch of the guys and I decided to pull a prank on him. The boys got together and asked him to join us. I came forward and told him that we had real reservations about coming clean to him about everything and if he wanted to know the whole story, he would have to prove his alliance to us. "How do you mean?" he asked. "I'll start with telling you that we smoke marijuana sometimes. That alone is telling you a lot," I said. "Okay," he responded. We could tell he was getting uncomfortable already, and his strange low voice was getting even lower. It was apparent he was a little frightened. Then I said, "If you smoke a joint with us, we will know for sure you are with us." He knew next to nothing about marijuana except that it was used to get high. With that, I took out a rolled joint, but it was full of oregano we stole from the kitchen. I lit it up, took a hit and handed it to him. It seemed to take minutes to get from his hand to his mouth as he was shaking so badly before it finally touched his lips. I could tell he didn't take a drag, so I told him to take another. Again, as frightened as he was, he put it to his lips and pretended to take a hit. He was between a rock and a hard place because he didn't want to lose his grant, but he was told that he was never going to be successful unless he did this. I think he shit his pants a little. It wasn't for 2 or 3 days before someone told him the truth. Boy, was he pissed at me! When his thesis was completed, his book became required reading for psychology students at Columbia University. He was truly a decent man and honest enough to write what really happened — even about the night with the so-called joint!

During my last year at Hawthorne, I met Alice Pelkey, one of the girls also "serving time" there who became my new girlfriend. Alice was 5'4", had long black hair, cute figure with a nice butt, and she wore dark-rimmed glasses that made her look smart. But like every other nice-looking girl there, she had that wild streak. The less attractive girls were much less outgoing and more reserved. In general, most of them

31

were more aggressive and sometimes a little violent. They would demand favors of the other girls like washing their clothes and doing their chores, or they'd physically push the other girls around or worse — very much like the boys, but not quite as violent. It was the same situation whereby we'd have someone pass my girlfriend a note for a clandestine late-night meet-up for a make-out session.

Alice had good grades at our school and was not considered a flight risk, so for those reasons she was allowed to attend a regular school off the premises. We were an item for a year until one night Flip DeVito said he wanted to talk and asked me to meet him in cottage 9. We entered through the side door because I wasn't announcing to the cottage "parents" I was there, and we made our way into the basement where the showers were. It was a place to go to get whacked, so to speak, because no one was there. Flip turns to me and says Harvey Booker has something to tell me regarding one of my buddies that I sang with, Mike Middleman. With that, he sends for Middleman. I had no idea what this was about until Flip pushed him into telling me that he too was seeing

Alice. They had met at an event and started making out. Middleman insisted it was only once, but the others insisted it was more. Middleman was a meek boy, and I couldn't see him doing that to me, his singing pal. He insisted it was Alice who was coming on to him, and I believed him knowing their personalities. Flip was looking for a brawl, but all I could do was push him. It wasn't in me to beat anyone. I didn't feel any rage; I guess it was never love, just ego.

Regardless of this situation, Alice asked me to her prom, and I accepted the invitation. It was near the end of my term at Hawthorne, so I received permission to attend. That would be the last time we would see each other. She graduated and left Hawthorne, and I left shortly thereafter.

Chapter Three

Can We Ever Go Home Again?

B y the end of the summer of 1957, I was turning 18 and would no longer be a ward of the state. The day had finally arrived when I would be released from this institution called a "reformatory" school, which should have been more appropriately called a junior prison. Dennis O'Shea, the same man that picked me up nearly three years prior when I first entered Hawthorne, offered me a ride to New York's Penn Station where I took the train to Long Beach. Mom and my oldest brother Arnie were the only two living at home at that time. My brother Norman was making a career in the Air Force, and my youngest brother, Robert, who had been living with my aunt and uncle, also ended up becoming a ward of the state (likely for being truant as well) and was shipped to George Junior Republic in Freeville, New York, where his closest friend became Johnny Crawford, son of the infamous mother and actress, Joan Crawford.

I was looking forward to becoming a part of a family again and having a natural parent, but what I longed for even more than that was being able to date. At 18, the only time I had any intimacy was a few clandestine meetings in the middle of the night at Hawthorne. What I really wanted was to have a normal girlfriend and a normal relationship like nearly everyone my age, but I had never even asked a girl out. With being away, I had missed out on those formative years: the Saturday night dates, making out with a girl at the movies and behind the bleachers, or walking someone home and meeting her parents. Because the boys in Hawthorne had been denied these events as well, there was no one at the school I could ask questions. I didn't know if I was supposed to just approach a random girl and ask for her phone number, or if there was a protocol to it all and maybe it was my job to find out first if she was interested in me. My experiences at Hawthorne had been with girls who were assertive and aggressive, but I was certain that was not the way all girls behaved and was apprehensive I would make a fool of myself.

Going back home was not exactly returning to normalcy; there was still nothing normal about my life. Not only was Dad gone, but the family had become largely dispersed. Being in a wheelchair, Mom was fortunate enough to have a good friend come for her each workday with his van. He would push her to the sidewalk, lift her, place her in the front seat, and then pack her wheelchair in the back. And at the end of the day, he would return her the same way. We considered him an angel I am sure sent by my father.

My brother Arnie was able to help me get my first job as a Good Humor man selling ice cream out of an icebox attached to a 3-wheeler bike. Once summer ended, I became a delivery boy for a cleaning service, then a delivery boy for a major drugstore chain, and finally a letter carrier until being promoted to a driver for our local post office, all within 12 months. One of the women in our neighborhood used all four delivery services, and by the time I showed up at her door wearing my fourth uniform, she thought she was becoming delusional.

With my newfound freedom, I would meet up with my old friend Ricky, and we would go to the boardwalk in town in the evenings to "people watch," eat boardwalk food, and play games in the arcades. Even with the backdrop of the Atlantic Ocean, the largest attraction was always the girls. Ricky loved to sing as much as I did, and we became a duo performing doo-wop on the boardwalk, eventually getting paid to sing at a local restaurant and nightclub. Not only was I doing what I loved the most, but we were attracting girls, and quickly my biggest fear of asking a girl out became unrealized. As it turned out, all I had to do was sing!

That is where I met Carol, a cute 16-year-old blonde who also loved singing. With our love of music, she quickly became a good friend and was always available when I needed a ride. Having newly divorced parents, she was living with her father in town and had freedom unlike other teenage girls her age. I enjoyed her company, and we soon became friends with benefits. That is also when I met the incomparable Freddie Scott, a well-known, Black club singer. Together the four of us formed the group *The Symphonics* with Freddie as the lead singer, and Carol, Ricky and I singing backup. We performed at the Baby

Grand in New York City's Harlem district and in Brooklyn with such acts as Redd Foxx and Nipsey Russell. In the smaller clubs, I also played the keyboard for the group. In addition to singing with the group, Freddie and I would travel the "Chitlin Circuit" performing together for Black audiences in Pennsylvania and New York. When I wanted to go to Atlanta with him to perform, he told me it was too dangerous for a white boy to go with him, stating, "They'd hang me first!"

Years later I would also perform with Claude "Sonny" Johnson, lead singer of *The Genies*, after he wrote and sang the hit song "Who's That Knocking." Sonny eventually became half of the duo, *Don & Juan*, and had the hit single "What's Your Name," while Freddie would also have great success with his hit song, "Hey, Girl" the very same year.

On my 19th birthday, Uncle Irving generously gifted me a 1949 Mercury and paid the first year's insurance. "The Green Hornet," as it was called, was equipped with skirts and dual exhaust and appeared to be a true hot rod, but, in actuality, it could never get over 50 mph. By then, Mom returned to a rehabilitation center, and I made the decision to move in with Ricky. That was when I became an entrepreneur. We started to run poker games from our apartment every Friday and Saturday night that went on from 11 p.m. to 5 a.m., earning Ricky and I $150-$200 a piece each night with our cut of the pot. I was doing so well, I quit my job at the post office. But within a year I became disillusioned with staying up all night and moved in with my other singing pal Freddie Scott and his girlfriend Lil who lived in one of the homes my father built, while Ricky moved in with his new girlfriend. Freddie and Lil were my kind of people. I loved so many things about their Black culture: their clothing, their dance moves, their fun expressions, but mostly I loved their music; it had soul. They could take a simple song and make it much more expressive. We learned that the best place to practice was in the men's bathroom at the Long Beach train station because the acoustics were outstanding, our voices bouncing off the high tiled ceiling and walls, echoing back to us, and when the harmony was right between us, the music sounded like it was coming from heaven. But my life would change yet again when Carol called to inform me that she was pregnant!

Stunned over the news, I was speechless because I thought she was using some form of birth control. When I asked how far along the pregnancy was, she claimed she did not know exactly. When further pressed, she admitted to being over four months along and stated she wanted to keep the baby and raise it together. By then I was spending a lot more time in midtown Manhattan hoping to establish a singing career, so I moved us into a hotel in the city and obtained a job as a counterman at Howard Johnsons. But I knew at 19 years old I was not ready to marry anyone or be a father. I still made every effort to take care of us financially, but I was barely earning enough to support myself alone. Within a month or two, Carol moved into her mother's apartment, and soon thereafter she went to live in a home for unwed mothers in Staten Island where our baby girl was placed for adoption with a Jewish family. We were instructed by the agency to never think about the baby going forward and to go on with our lives as if it never happened. I had mixed emotions about all of it, about giving up my own flesh and blood, but I knew the baby deserved more than what I could give her. I visited Carol at the home once, but it would be many years before I would see her or the baby again.

I stayed in New York where I met Daisy, a professional skier from Switzerland who invited me to live with her in her third-floor walk-up in Manhattan. She was sweet but plain compared to American girls and barely spoke a word of English. But after a year, I was bored with our inability to communicate and told her I was planning to move out. Blaming herself for being too plain, for not being a "painted girl," she attempted to coerce me into staying, declaring she would become more Americanized. When I returned to pick up the last of my belongings, she greeted me all made up but looking more like a clown than a classy New Yorker that I was embarrassed for her. Her feeble attempt made me feel even more beastly, and I tried to convince her it had nothing to do with her being unpretentious.

I was hanging in New York's most popular clubs like the Wagon Wheel, the Peppermint Lounge, the Latin Quarter, and the Copacabana and got to know the employees, especially the dancers. Just like the Broadway dancers, the girls wore heavy make-up with exaggerated eye lashes, loud enough for the people in the back of the room to see. During the break between a show one evening at the Latin Quarter, the lead dancer, still in the show's full garb, asked me to walk with her to the Strand Bar a few blocks away. As luck would have it, I was mortified to see Daisy only 40 feet away from us. From the looks of things with the dancer and me, Daisy was correct in her belief that I was leaving her for a "painted woman." It had only been a few weeks since I moved out of her apartment, and I could see the anger in her face even at that distance. I stopped and attempted to mouth to her, "It's not a girlfriend; only a dancer," but she hurried away. I wanted to go after her and explain, but she was with a guy, and I did not want to create a problem for her. I may not have loved Daisy but hurting her like that was upsetting to me.

It was the late 1950s when drugstores served food and soft drinks like chocolate egg creams (a beverage made at a soda counter) that were indigenous to New York City. A favorite spot to go was Whelan's Drug Store on 47th & Broadway where the food counters were long, and the girls were plentiful. There you could not only buy your medical supplies, but also pick up a hooker at the counter on your way out. At 5'2", an unprepossessing, heavyset white woman they called "Broadway Rose" was their madam. A guy would approach Rose and ask how much for a specific girl — prices ranging from $30 to $50, depending on the girl. The prostitute would keep two-thirds of the price. Rose not only controlled her women, but also her little Black boyfriend we would often see walking her little white poodle. They were a frightening sight themselves.

I was still making every effort to establish myself in the music world, recording a few records with *The Symphonics* and the original *Honey & the Bees*, and hung out in that part of the city hoping to rub shoulders with the great singers and their musicians. But my counterman job was not earning me much, and sometimes I would have to give up my hotel room and swap it out for a friend's couch. Much of the time, when it was not convenient for a friend to have an overnight guest, I slept in the back seat of my Sunbeam Talbot for as long as a week at a time and showered at a friend's place.   As time went on and I became more frustrated with my financial situation, I reverted to my "street" ways. I could never rob or hurt anyone, but I teamed up with Broadway Rose by procuring more women and received a cut of what they made from their johns. I never liked the way some of my street brothers picked up girls and brought them into "the life." My friend Pee Wee attempted to teach me the pimp business, but I never wanted to emulate him; It was not my style to deceive anyone. He would go to the Greyhound bus station and Port Authority looking for runaways. He could spot them by the way they looked around, not being familiar with the place, walking around aimlessly and carrying a suitcase. He would approach a young girl and attempt to start a conversation by saying, "Hi, my name is Pee Wee (already getting their attention), and I am a New York guide. Do you need a cab, hotel, or someone to show you around?" If she responded positively in any way, he would ask her if he could buy her a cup of coffee. This is where he would find out why she was there, how ugly her life at home was. When he learned the dirty facts, he would continue his pitch if the girl did not know anyone in the city because that would most likely create a big problem for him. He would tell them, "The hotels in New York are very expensive, but you can use my place tonight; I don't even sleep there." About one-third of the time, the girls were so desperate or scared, they would take him up on his offer. The pimps were proficient at knowing who looked like a runaway. Once he brought them to his place, he would leave and then return a few hours later. If she were in bed, he would make a move on her. If she declined his advances, he was not forceful at that point. He would make every effort to befriend her and make her feel welcome the first few days, and if he were successful and became intimate with her, which was about 75% of the time, he began to show his true colors. He convinced them that he could be their "everything" — their lover, friend, father, protector — in an attempt to make her feel secure and convince her he had given up other women for her. His next move would be to introduce her to one of his other girls as a friend by taking them dancing so she would get more comfortable with him. Or, he would take her for a walk to where one of his girls was working a corner, and when a car approached the woman, he'd say, "She's going to make a lot of money tonight. She's a classy chick, and the guys just love her." Every word, every gesture he made was to feel her out.

Sometimes, after a few days, he would stage a robbery of the apartment which would leave her with no money at all. He would claim that he, too, was robbed and continue telling her tales of how dangerous the city was and how the police did not care, instilling her with more fear and greater desperation than she had when she first arrived. That was when he started to suggest that she have sex for money, telling her that she, too, was classy and could make a great deal of money. "Just do it this once," he would say. Of course, it was never just once. When she would ask for her cut of the deal, he would tell her that the money was in a joint account and not to worry; he was taking care of everything. If the pimp did hard drugs, he would persuade her into trying heroin. Once that began, she was going nowhere. If she threatened to leave, that was when he would start to get physical and threaten her. He would tell her that HE gave up everything for her and she gave up nothing! "You came here not knowing anything. You do not know how dangerous it is out there. I saved you!" But I would not hang out at the bus or railway stations to solicit women. The women I introduced to Broadway Rose were women I met in passing and never had to coerce. I earned just enough to help pay my hotel bill.

At 2 a.m. one morning, I walked into a diner and was greeted by an acquaintance named Frosty who I had been introduced to at the Wagon Wheel by the house bandleader, Bobby Jay, and his drummer, Frankie Vincent, who would later become a reputable actor. When I met Frosty, she had been dating Bobby Jay but was now available. At 5'2," blue eyes, blonde hair, and shapely, she was beautiful. That night, or morning, she invited me to join her at her table. When we were done, we walked over to my hotel, and as Frosty perused my bleak living space with merely two hangers of clothing, I explained that my car had been broken into and the suitcases stolen. All I had left to my name were those two hangers containing a pair of jeans, a shirt, and a jacket. With that, she instructed me to take my few belongings and move in with her that same evening. There was, however, a big caveat.

Frosty was occupying a suite in an upscale hotel on 33rd Street that was being paid for by her married sugar daddy, a shoe magnate. The suite was as large as some people's homes, decorated like a homey residence with paintings adorning the walls and her personal knickknacks and photographs on the tables. Her clothes packed the closets with over a hundred pairs of shoes strewn throughout. When her lover visited, he would shower her with bags of shoes, bags, and accessories.

Frosty explained that he visited her several times a week after work, and during those hours, I would need to be out of the apartment. Having so little clothing, it was not difficult to conceal my presence. What her sugar daddy also didn't know was that Frosty had two other johns. Regardless, I quickly fell in love with her and did not have a problem with her business, especially since I was living quite well because of her. But she hated me working with Broadway Rose or at my counterman job and tried to prevent me from doing so by always requesting that I accompany her to her appointments where I would wait in a nearby bar until she was finished with her john. I knew she had no feelings for these men, and during the hours she was not with them, we had a genuinely nice life.

A few months passed when I ran into a friend who invited me to go boating with him. Frosty had quickly gotten used to me taking her to appointments, so when I told her that I would be going out with a friend one afternoon, she tried to stop me by giving me an ultimatum. I did not do well with threats as it was, and I certainly was not going to be tossed around by her or anyone else. When I returned that night to her suite, I thought I had entered the wrong room. Every single piece of clothing and every possession she had was gone, and all that was left were my two clothes hangers. I learned that she called her shoe john to move her out, and he sent several limos to pick her and her belongings up. I was devastated; no one had ever hurt me that like before, and my heart went cold.

A few months would pass before I saw her again on the street. She told me she had been too harsh that day and asked if we could get back together. But after the way she left me, I no longer felt the same way and declined her offer.

Freddie had a gig to sing at an outdoor festival in Harlem on their main drag, 125th Street, near the famous Apollo Theater. Freddie's new wife and I were his backup singers. The corner was packed with thousands of people perched on the bleachers set up for the occasion and lining the streets for blocks. Five acts had performed before we took the stage. Freddie was singing "Last Train to Jacksonville" and wowing the crowd when someone lifted his arm pointing to the sky and shot off a gun as if starting a race. Immediately everyone started to run in all directions. After a minute or two, Freddie calmly spoke into the microphone telling everyone to relax and that it was just a firecracker, when another man in the crowd yelled out, "Firecracker, bullshit. This is Harlem; it was a gun!"

That was the last year the festival took place in Harlem.

After some time, I started living near Central Park in New York City with a woman named Pam — a waitress I met at the Peppermint Lounge, a club that became very popular for its house band, *Joey Dee & the Starliters*. We remained in New York for a year before moving to Miami together. By then, I was 23 years old and had given up pursuing the dream of becoming a big singer. Although Pam had been a former schoolteacher, she decided to keep working in a restaurant, both of us taking jobs waiting tables at different establishments. Over the year, we fought more and saw less of each other. Pam loved to smoke marijuana, and our lives became consumed with waiting tables and getting high. As it turned out, it was the worst time for me to leave New York and the music business: It was 1963, and Freddie and Sonny both released their hit songs that made the Billboard top ten ... without me.

My mother's sister was visiting Miami for the winter and staying at a hotel near us. Several times a week I would visit her and together have lunch in the hotel's restaurant. My aunt was proud of the way I looked and the ease at which I could converse with a total stranger. But she had one crazy habit: She introduced me to everyone as her nephew, the "doctor"! To my knowledge, most people never caught on that they were being totally bullshitted, and I was fortunate they never asked a medical question. Then one afternoon, she introduced me to a woman, also from New York, at a nearby table, as, again, her nephew, the doctor. With that, the woman whips out her wallet to show me a photo of her daughter she was hoping to introduce to me when she arrived in a few days. Considering they were there for the winter, too, we would certainly meet.

It was only a few days before that woman kept her promise. Lynn was as cute as the photo, 5'2", eyes of blue, and shapely. We started to date even though I was still living with Pam, and I told Lynn from the beginning what my real occupation was. She responded, "Just don't tell my parents — yet." I knew immediately she was not like the other girls I dated. She was a "good girl," not flashy or a game player, she didn't sleep around or do drugs, and she was Jewish. As soon as I met her, I knew my mother would approve. My life was going nowhere with Pam or any of the other girls I had lived with. Lynn was from the type of family I had as a young kid and wanted again.

52

And, luckily, Lynn had liked me enough to drop her standards from dating a physician to a waiter.

The winter was ending, and she, like the rest of the snowbirds, were leaving to return north. Pam and I were returning to New York; she was going to the apartment we shared that had been subleased, and I informed her I was moving in with a friend. Unbeknownst to her, that friend was Lynn *and* her family. That would be when Lynn's parents would also learn my true occupation.

Chapter Four

Market Day

D riving nonstop those interminable 1,300 miles from Miami to New York City, Pam and I continued to argue over what our life together had become, making for a most miserable and uncomfortable journey. But when I told her that I was not moving back into the apartment and that I was going to live with a friend, she didn't carry on — she merely became quiet.

I wasn't leaving because I met Lynn — it was because my life was going nowhere with Pam. All we ever did was smoke marijuana and fight when we weren't working. I imagined my mature self as I saw my dad, a successful husband, father, and businessman, but most of all, a happy man, happy with his life. I possessed none of that yet.

When we arrived at our New York City apartment, we walked into the unit together, and I gathered the last of my belongings. She never tried to stop me from walking out nor did she try to even converse with me. She knew it was over, and I left her forever with a simple good-bye. No drama whatsoever. That would be the last time I would end a relationship unceremoniously — the very last time!

I walked out of the front door 10 minutes after walking in, and when I exited the building, Lynn was there to retrieve me. While driving back to New York from Florida, Lynn had the dreaded conversation with her parents — you know, the one where you tell your parents that the love of your life is a waiter and not a doctor like they had been told. That one. Lynn's father did not approve given the change of events, but she explained it was not me who lied to them; it had always been my aunt. She skillfully convinced them that I was smart, ambitious, and a hard worker and persuaded them into believing she had a future with me, but what I believe had them acquiesce to me moving in was her pronouncement that I was the love of her life. Dolefully, her parents resigned themselves to the circumstances and conceded to their daughter's wishes.

I moved into their den that afternoon.

The very next day I was given a job as assistant manager for John's Bargain Store located immediately around the corner from the apartment. Within two weeks, I secured my own apartment in the same neighborhood and, shortly thereafter, sought for a better opportunity in sales working for E.J. Corvettes Carpeting and Allen Carpeting where I learned to develop my sales skills that would carry me my entire career. Within a year, Lynn and I were engaged.

It was 1965 and I was taking a train to see Freddie Scott's brother-in-law, Roland, in Harlem at the Spot Lounge and pick up a bag of weed. The last time we saw each other we ended the evening late, and Roland invited me to stay the night. The following morning two of the cutest little kids came into the room and asked if I wanted grits for breakfast. Never having eaten them, I thought I'd try and answered them, "I'll have a few." When the kids returned to their mother in the kitchen, I could hear the laughter all the way to my room.

Getting out of the subway, I started my eight-block walk up Lenox Avenue to the lounge. I've made this walk a hundred times, but this time was different. It was unusual for a white guy to be casually walking through Harlem like I always did, saying hello to everyone I passed. Everyone nodded or repeated hello back. And when I arrived at the lounge, the bartender knew what I drank and delivered one to me when I sat down. He didn't know my name, but he knew my drink. But on this day, no one would even look at me the entire eight blocks.

Instead of the bartender immediately delivering my drink when I arrived, he ignored me. So did the eight other customers. It was 10 long minutes before Roland walked in and broke the silence. He signaled the bartender for our drinks, and only then did he deliver mine, never looking at me. I explained to Roland that it had been an odd day and he said, "Something is going on with racial rioting that started in Watts, California, and is now here."

One of the customers turns to Roland and said, "What's up?" referring to me.

"Everything's cool," Roland replied.

"You know what's going on!" (Meaning, what the fuck are you doing with that white boy?) "Why are you shielding him?"

"That's my business; he's with me," Roland snapped back.

The customer responded, "You know I saved your life way back? Maybe you owe me one?"

I never asked what "owing him" meant as it referred to me, but I assumed he was at least expecting him to beat the shit out of me.

Instead of Roland backing down, he fired back assertively, "Well, don't save me again."

"Oh, it's like that?" the customer replied.

"Yeah, it's just like that."

Roland then told me to take my time finishing my drink so I wouldn't look afraid, and he'd inform me when we would make the move. As we left the bar, he instructed me to not turn and look back. Once outside, he hailed a cab for me.

I had hung out with my Black friends, lived with them, sang with them, and thought of them as my family. I never saw color — until that day. They had made it abundantly clear we were not brothers. It would be another year before I returned to Harlem.

A year after getting engaged, Lynn and I married and moved into an apartment building in Spring Valley, NY. Within a year of our marriage, Lynn became pregnant with our first child.

When Lynn reached her seventh month of pregnancy, her asthma began to flare up, but not to the extent we considered it was affecting the baby. At eight months, the bedroom was decorated and ready for our new arrival. Then, in the middle of the night that month, Lynn could not catch her breath, and we hurriedly left for the hospital. Walking down the front steps, our neighbor excitedly yelled out, "Good Luck," expecting to see us return with a baby wrapped in a blue or pink blanket in five days.

Lynn was given a cesarean section and delivered a baby girl that night. But the doctors knew immediately that the lack of oxygen from the asthma attacks did, in fact, affect the baby. Her head was disproportionate in size. I was merely told that there were complications with clearing the baby's lungs and that her head was enlarged, but I still expected the hospital to be able to clear her lungs and receive positive results. I was expecting to take them both home! In the meantime, I roamed the hospital corridors, lobby, and sat at Lynn's side while she slept and waited to hear that our baby was out of the woods.

Finally, after eight hours, the delivering physician informed me that the hospital did not have the necessary equipment to help my baby beyond that point and was not expecting her to survive. He asked if I wanted to let the baby just die or attempt to get her help by transporting her to another hospital. In disbelief of the crudeness in which this "life" was being regarded, I instructed him to take whatever measures necessary to save her. An ambulance was ordered, but just when she was being placed into the vehicle, she succumbed to her illness. She had lived only nine hours.

Upon learning of her passing, the physician further stunned me by asking if I wanted to "destroy the remains," as if she never existed, or if I wanted to give my daughter a proper funeral. She was our flesh and blood, and she did exist! We gave her a proper funeral and named her Timi after Timi Yuro who recorded a song I co-wrote with Freddie Scott.

In early 1967, a year after losing our first baby, Lynn became pregnant again, and this time we switched physicians and delivered the baby at Mount Sinai Hospital, and neither Lynn nor the baby suffered from any asthma attacks. The second baby girl was born 12 months after the first, and like her late sister, we named her Timi.

It wasn't long before I was able to purchase our first home in an upscale neighborhood of Rockland County and kept Lynn's promise to her parents by providing for their daughter even better than they had. Two years later, my wife gave birth to our son, Damon.

By the time I turned 30, I had achieved the American dream and would have made my own father proud.

One of Lynn's cousins recommended me for an outside sales position in the garment industry, and it was there that I started to earn decent money with a "big boy" sales position soliciting clothing stores. The job offered me the kind of autonomy only a sales position could. On Tuesdays, known in the industry as "market day," all the salesmen in the business reported to their offices in Manhattan. It was the one day of the week when customers could come by with returns, to have a conversation with the bosses, get to see a new style or to make purchases. The salesmen came into the offices for meetings and to be there when their customers were at the office. It was the same for everyone in the garment center. After our meetings, the salesmen would meet for dinner at a restaurant or a hotel where I would meet up with my buddies in the industry whom I had known from my younger days in the Bronx. Inevitably, at least one of the guys would bring one or two of the models from his showroom.

It was the early 70s, and everyone I knew in the business was sleeping around, especially on market day. It all began innocently enough. After dinner and a few drinks, the models and the guys would always start to get it on. It would start in the restaurant or in one of the guy's hotel suites. Already liquored up, it very quickly evolved into a well-formed orgy, as if it were a long-planned bachelor party. But there was no planning of any kind, and no one seemed to care if anyone was married, who they were naked in front of, who was watching them, and sometimes whose penis slipped into their vagina. No one cared; IT WAS TUESDAY.

One Tuesday night, my buddies picked a Mexican restaurant. There were eight of us, and when I arrived, my friend Freddy asked if I wanted to meet a model from his office. She lived in the direction of my home, and Freddy asked if I would drive her home at the end of the evening. I agreed, and we were paired together. We all started drinking tequila, something I had never done before, and it wasn't long before the tequila was doing me. I was never a big drinker, my vice of choice was marijuana, not exactly a hard drug, but little did I know this drink would hit me like a poisonous snake.

The model was tall, thin, and beautiful, certainly pleasant enough to get to know. As the evening progressed, we ate dinner at which time a second tequila was bestowed upon me. It wasn't long before my stomach writhed. Running one flight down to the men's room, I made it to the toilet, but not without some of the remains of my masticated dinner on my jacket. I was able to clean myself off in the men's sink and began to feel recovered after releasing my dinner into the toilet. Some cold water to my face, rinse my mouth, fingers through my hair, and I'm back to the party, so, I thought. I was profoundly ignorant of this liquor, to say the least.

It all went fine until it didn't. I became all too confident and arrogantly continued with the tequila. It wasn't long before my stomach started to squirm again, but this time there would be no lead time. I never made it anywhere near the men's room and ended up regurgitating my dinner right there at our table! This time, my jacket took a bigger hit, and no amount of men's room sink water was going to make me smell anything better than a sewer.

An hour later, the model gets into my car and I drive her home safely! She sat so far away from me that she was almost out the window. I'm sure she was praying to make it home without me vomiting all over her. When we arrived at her home, she couldn't get out of the car fast enough. I never saw her again. You could say I left a lasting impression on her.

I was offered a part-time sales position selling encyclopedias. I was able to make the sales calls in the evenings and not affect my work in the garment center. But, within a short period of time, I was earning enough income to quit my full-time position, and I exchanged the garment world, aka "the Tuesday world," for the book world, aka "the real world." But Tuesdays were never so far behind.

We were having trouble with a distributor, and it became necessary for me to work that summer in Erie, PA, over 400 miles from home. Before arriving, however, I made a few sales calls on the way down. I was in Buffalo when a great looking, short-haired blonde about 15 years my junior appeared at one of the doors. I explained why I was there and that wanted to meet with her parents who were inquiring about the program. She invited me into the home, and I proceeded to give her my shortened sales pitch. In conversation, I mentioned how I'd be leaving to go to Erie for the summer and wanted to see what her parents decided before leaving Buffalo. Friendly and a little flirtatious as she was, I still never considered anything except the potential sale. I left her home that day with merely a reminder to call back.

Two days later when I followed up on the appointment with Blondie's parents, Blondie herself answered the phone. She informed me that she discussed the program with her parents, but that they weren't interested. However, though, she explained how she had been thinking of **moving** to Erie to be with some friends and asked if I would mind driving her.

So, on my way out of Buffalo, I picked up Blondie and drove 1 ½ hours to our destination in Erie. She had arranged to meet her friends at a bar there who were hooking her up with an apartment. When we arrived at the bar, I immediately recognized the band leader from the Peppermint Lounge in Manhattan, and he recognized me after nearly two decades. It could not have been a more perfect place for me; they were the house band and were performing nearly every night. From that moment on, that bar became my go-to place that summer where I drank, ate, and sang several times a week.

My first few days of residency in Erie were spent with Blondie at the apartment her friends arranged. Our first night together was spent having sex; our second night was spent swapping partners with the bandleader and his most recent lay. After that weekend, to Blondie's acute disappointment, I moved in with one of my salesmen. Because Blondie and I had friends at the same bar, we ended up hanging in the same circle, although she continued to remain mad at me for leaving her. I never did ask what she expected of me. I was merely giving her a ride, and she was contemplating a more permanent situation. All from one fucking ride!

Never once did she ask if I was married. I never mentioned it either.

Within two years of entering the book industry and the encouragement of my CPA and good friend, Anthony, I was financially able to start my own business selling children's learning programs after discovering that my boss was stealing commissions from the salesmen. I was successful coming out of the gate, beginning as a one-man operation, and quickly expanding into different states where I needed to hire and train salespeople and managers. Lynn was a happy homemaker while I was out on the road making money. She had free rein with anything related to the house, and my absence became commonplace. When I hired a new guy to sell or a manager to open a new office anywhere in the states, I got to know him well. In the evenings, I would typically accompany them on a sales call to see how they were selling the product, and after the appointments each night we would inevitably stop in a bar or restaurant that had music, many of them karaoke joints where I got to do what I loved the most — sing! Life was good.

Every Christmas vacation, we did what every other American Jew did: We drove to Miami. It was the law. On the last day of school, we would pack into our van and drive the 1300 miles non-stop — Timi and I in the front seat talking to truckers through the night on our CB radio, while Lynn and Damon slept in the back seat. We would arrive at Lynn's parent's home just before Christmas Day and leave after the new year.

Upon arrival, her mother would so proudly announce the prodigious amount of food awaiting us, a list of at least 25 items, before inquiring what the kids wanted to eat. If the kids requested item #16 on the list, she would respond, "Oh, that's for Thursday's dinner." Then, after they'd made their second selection, item #21, she'd mournfully respond, "That's for Tuesday." We never had the right day and settled for what she wanted us to have. It annoyed me, but this was Lynn's family, and I let it go until one day I didn't.

Lynn's mom wasn't only frugal, she was controlling. Passing through the kitchen late one night after her parents retired to bed, I made the cardinal sin of opening her refrigerator and filching about six grapes. The following morning at breakfast several items were discussed, and then, bam, she hits me with, "By the way, Preston, did you take any grapes last night?" With that, I instructed Lynn and the kids to pack their belongings, and we checked into a hotel that afternoon. My mother-in-law never tried to stop me, nor did she ever apologize.

It wasn't until our lavish 25th wedding anniversary party held on the World Yacht that Lynn's father professed in front of everyone how wrong he had been about me all those years.

By the time my kids were just reaching high-school age, I was able to purchase a large second home in Boca Raton, Florida, on a beautiful golf course, The Polo Club. Lynn, a graduate of MIT, became passionate about redesigning and decorating it. During our entire marriage, I was Lynn's one and only client. For what I paid, she didn't need others.

In addition to owning a second home in Florida, I had a salesman there working the territory, and both my mother and my eldest brother Arnie were living there. My mother was in a nursing home financed by me, and Arnie was divorced and living alone. I would fly down periodically to see everyone, especially my mother, and would handle her affairs when necessary. When the conditions in the nursing home became unacceptable, I moved her to another one. Her complaints were never further than a phone call away to me.

My freedom afforded me the opportunity to have two lives: one married and one single. Sex was still easily available. In a bar, I didn't approach women, they approached me. They were normally in a group, and I would end up taking the cutest one back to their home and screw her. I'd meet new women everywhere and anywhere. In a gas station one evening heading home, a young girl started a conversation with me, and the next thing you know we're having sex in my car. In an effort to get me to go home with her, she told me how she liked to fall asleep with a dick in her mouth. I told her I'd follow her, but when the exit came up, I went in the opposite direction to my own home. They didn't care if I had a wedding band on or not. If they wanted to get laid, they weren't shy about it. But never once did I ever consider leaving my family and never was it portrayed that way. An easy lay was merely an easy lay. It didn't matter what they wanted from me except an erect

71

penis that night; no one was getting more. It wasn't my love life at home keeping me there, it was my kids, and I wasn't about to change that. Lynn had been kind enough to me as well as a good mother to our kids, but there hadn't been flames between us, no real affection. Not what my parents had. As extroverted as I was, she was introverted; as optimistic as I was, she was pessimistic. But we seldom fought, I was free to work and play, and our bank account afforded us both an extremely comfortable living.

The only time my other life became a problem was when I stopped sleeping with a married woman in her mid-twenties who wanted more from me. Wild and aggressive, she had already been banging two of my friends, brothers, but wanted me. Considering she, too, was married AND screwing my friends, I thought it was a safe relationship. After I stopped seeing her, she telephoned me weeks later asking if I'd join her on a three-day vacation in the Bahamas, all expenses paid. I was already planning on heading south that weekend to my Florida home, so I decided a few days later to take her up on her offer; at the end of the trip, I'd have a short flight to my second home where Lynn was. But when we returned home, she wanted to resume our relationship, and I said it was not going to work. The next phone call from her merely said, "Call your home." She had phoned my house deliberately to tell Lynn about our tryst.

I was in St. Louis and staying with my nephew whom I had relocated to open an office there. I was sitting in the park waiting for one of my salesmen one hot summer's afternoon, when I came upon a guy shooting basketballs alone before he invited me to join him. Never being one to pass up a conversation or a basketball match, we played for about a full hour with a few small breaks when my heart could not stop racing. I sat for a while with no change in the rapidity of my heart beats, and when my basketball buddy asked if I was alright, I lied and said yes. About 10 minutes later I left the park and drove 15 minutes to the apartment where my nephew called EMS. It was then that I was diagnosed with my first heart attack; I had played much too hard and too long in an insalubrious climate. Lynn offered to fly out, but I told her to stay home with the kids, and I resumed my life as usual within a few days.

I enjoyed great relationships with both my kids. I may have been on the road often, but I remained involved in their lives and was consistent with the way I handled them: easy-going, always humorous about life and any event. I gave my kids a lot of leeway, always trusted them, and in return, luckily, they always did the right thing.

One day my son surprised me by inviting me out for a drink. At 19 years old, handsome as any movie star, and like me, a keyboard player and gifted singer, we had performed together at different events beginning with his bar mitzvah six years prior. Seated at the bar, he surreptitiously looked around and pointed out an attractive couple.

"Dad, do you see that couple there?"

I paused, wondering where this conversation was going before I replied, "Yeah."

"Well … I don't know who I would want to take home, the guy or the girl," he said almost mournfully.

"Are you gay?" I asked, calmly.

"I'm talking to a psychologist about this; I may not be," he explained.

Remaining calm, I replied, "Do you think you might want to take the guy home?"

"Yes."

"Then, Damon, you're gay!"

"But my psychologist says I may not be."

"Damon, maybe save your money on that shrink. I know the answer. If I'm at a bar and I see an attractive couple, I KNOW who I want to take home! If you are, you are; there's nothing wrong."

I could see the release of tension dissipate from him like a hot air balloon rising into the heavens until it was invisible. I genuinely felt relieved. He was always a good son, but he suffered with angst, and now this explained a great deal. I was actually happy he had found out who he really was and what had been the problem all along, and all that anxiety was suddenly understandable.

The segment of the book industry I was in was small, and all the companies obtained their sales leads the same way: through various private schools that we loosely cultivated a relationship with. For the families responding to the inquiries, there was a need for the program 100 percent of the time. And nearly 100 percent of the time it came down to money. There were no big bells or whistles. Work the program 10 minutes a day and you will learn something. It was legit. But it was difficult to get salesmen. Difficult to get, and difficult to keep. The appointments were only nights and weekends, and it was a one-shot close. If the salesman couldn't close the sale at the appointment, there was no making money at all. The sales leads were valuable, and it was essential that you had a manager who could "place" schools and a person who could turn them into appointments. You worked every lead.

Before starting my own business, I worked with a salesman named Richard. He was a big, heavyset guy, broad muscular build, and very average looking. An only child of an educated family had afforded him a somewhat privileged upbringing, but Rich lacked social skills — although not enough to eliminate him from employment. He had this air of superiority and could be condescending all too easily. He loved to talk, and he loved to brag — mostly because he loved listening to himself. But he was alone on that mental island.

We were having some very profitable years and living the good life in upscale neighborhoods. As loquacious as Rich was, he was a man of few words at the appointments. Business was business, and it was all about the Benjamins. He delivered a straight, short speech, was convincing, and was able to earn a living at it. If a salesperson had an appointment with a lead generated by Rich, Rich, too, would make a commission on their sales close to the amount the salesperson was earning himself. Rich's most valuable quality was his unalarming presentation to the nuns (who were the source of all income) with his wardrobe that he had down to a science: long sleeve shirt, tie, khaki pants, and a sports jacket. If the nun agreed to hand out our flyer to their families, those leads that were converted into sales were paid a commission to him as well. He was doing the jobs of placing the schools and doing in-home sales as well, earning both ways. Unique and difficult to replace in the industry.

One day Rich appeared at my office asking for a job. He was desperate. My only concern was the leads he obtained while working for our previous employer, Lester. I told Richard I didn't want to get involved with them, and what he did with those leads was his decision. But Richard proceeded to create such a problem for me, Lester and I ended up fighting it out in court for years.

What Richard did that started Lester's rage was insert blank pieces of paper on the packages he received back from the nuns so that it was not immediately obvious that the "deck" was empty. It wasn't until the pile was retrieved to be worked on that they saw the leads were replaced with blank pieces of paper. Infuriated, Lester filed a suit against me that extended into two trials. I was sued on the grounds that I violated a non-compete clause by hiring him. I could never have imagined the set of circumstances that would evolve from this one hire.

Both my kids were adults at that time, only Timi was living at home, and Lynn decided she was going to live in Florida for a few months. I saw that she felt unneeded at home with the kids grown. I neither encouraged nor discouraged her decision to go, but little did I know how long she would be gone. My business headquarters was located near my first home, and if I wasn't there, my income suffered. With Lynn gone, I had every night free, and I knew every place that had singing within a 20-mile radius.

But after seven months of my wife beginning her sabbatical from our marriage and never returning to our first home, I made the decision to keep the split permanent. I had recently met someone and no longer wanted to run around or lie anymore. I booked a flight to West Palm Beach and asked Lynn to pick me up at the airport to tell her I wanted a permanent separation.

Seeing Lynn after such an absence was awkward for us both. Our telephone conversations were shorter, and after what she did next, I suspect Lynn was suspicious of my visit. Instead of driving us directly to our home, she inexplicitly took a detour to the beach, something very much out of her character. Silently sitting in the sand in our street clothes for some time, Lynn began a conversation about how she wanted things to change between us. Somewhat stunned and taken aback that she would even broach the subject in this way, I immediately came clean and said it was not going to work out. I made it understood that I wanted to stay apart permanently and live as single people. I wasn't looking for anything more; I merely wanted to remain separated. That was when I made the colossal mistake of telling my wife the truth: I told her I met someone while she was estranged from me.

In keeping with her character, Lynn became silent and expressed no emotions, no surprise, no anger, no rage, nothing. We got back into the car and drove to the condo, still in silence. I was staying for a week because my kids were flying down, and I also had made plans to visit a long-time friend, Anthony, to see his new home in the area. Lynn was invited and agreed to go along. While viewing Anthony's place, Lynn took the opportunity to speak, surreptitiously, to

Anthony's new wife, telling her that if she confided in scandalous acts of mine, then Lynn would confide in indiscretions of her husband's. Lynn's mind was obviously in divorce-lawyer mode already, and she was determined to get every conceivable morsel of information against me. Rifling through my wallet the following day, Lynn finds a photo of a woman, and I would soon learn that she immediately hired an attorney.

Before leaving Florida, I met up with a good "friend" and neighbor of ours, who was only too happy, you might even say joyous, to talk to me about Lynn. Unguardedly, Lynn had become close to this woman, confiding in her about an affair she was having with our house painter. I got to know this guy when we first purchased the home. Little did I know exactly how friendly he had become with my wife. As if our "friend" was repeating gossip about another couple in the neighborhood with the enthusiasm of an attorney advising me we had all the evidence we needed to destroy my wife, she then **confides in me** exactly how Linda was hiding his vehicle from the neighbors. And why was "our" friend so joyous to tell me? Because her own husband walked out on her after obtaining information of her sleeping around, and she was hoping to resurrect the few hook-ups WE had. More specifically, she was hoping I'd leave my wife for her. But that was never going to happen. She was just another easy lay, and leaving Lynn was never considered or discussed with her. It was all her hopes.

Regardless, there I was, supporting my wife's expensive lifestyle while she's screwing the hired help. Somewhat stunned, I knew we no longer had any reason to stay together. I remained married for over 25 years because I had no reason to leave. She was a good wife, honest, respectable, attractive, and a good mother, and I was never going to have my kids raised by another man. Being married to her was easy enough, as I came and went as I pleased. Rarely did she give me a problem about my late nights, and I didn't let the distraction of a fight with her upset my day when I had plans for a "liaison" that night — or day. As they say, I absolutely had my proverbial cake, and I ate it, too. The single feature that kept us together after the kids left was her fidelity. With that gone, we had nothing but a history.

Choose Your Friends, Choose Your Life

Chapter Five

Skateboarding Into Hell

After learning of Lynn's affair, I was committed to starting a new life, committed to being happy, to being in love, but mostly, I was committed to living a life without lies. I wanted to be free. I made every attempt to have an amicable divorce; Lynn would get the home in Florida, and I would keep the home in New York, splitting everything else. Fair, I thought. My kids were emancipated and given everything Lynn and I wanted to give them growing up, and as the years went by, I felt more and more as if I was being taken for granted by everyone in the family, especially since Lynn took a marriage sabbatical. I wanted to feel appreciated again. Mandy would fill that void. Eighteen years my junior, an attractive, single, unemployed mother, and a woman determined to pursue me.

Two weeks after returning from Florida and delivering the news to Lynn that I wanted to keep the separation permanent, I was sitting at my desk when the phone rang. My secretary announces, "Preston, it's Carol from Long Beach." Stunned, I hadn't spoken to Carol in 20 years. Happy to hear who was on the line, I quickly picked up.

For the first 15 to 20 minutes, we engaged merely in small talk, inquiring about our families, etc. Then she announced she had a reason for the call.

"Oh," I responded, laughing. "You found our daughter."

Carol giggled. "Well, no," hesitating, "but she found us."

Stunned, I replied, "Are you kidding?"

"No."

My mind reeling and always the joker, I replied, "Oh boy, what does she want? College money?"

"No, but she would like to meet you."

"Me? What about you?" I quickly responded.

"We've already met."

Carol explained that our daughter, named Beth, wrote her a beautiful letter assuring her that she understood if we did not want to meet her, further conveying she had no ill feelings about being placed for adoption. With a sense of great relief to me, Carol informed me that she grew up in a nice Jewish home, played piano, and "sings like you cannot believe."

"Do you want to speak to her?" Carol asked.

Hesitating, "No" I replied, "I want to meet her. I don't know what to say on the phone, so let's set up a meeting."

Within a week, a dinner for 20 was planned in New York City for the families to meet. And then I had to break the news to my kids that I had another child! I was actually excited to tell them; to me, they were getting another sibling to share their lives with. I guessed right with Damon, but not so with Timi!

For the first time, Timi and I were not getting along. She was living with me and speaking to her mother, putting her *square* in the middle at such a tumultuous time, and when I broke the news to her about a half-sister, it was more than she could handle. When the date for the dinner was arranged for the very next evening, I immediately asked Timi to join us. Uncharacteristic of her, she declined stating it was too much to deal with at that time. Had Damon been available to attend and give her emotional support, she likely would have accepted. I reassured Timi I was okay with her not attending and that I would invite someone else, just not disclosing it would be a woman I was dating. When asked, Mandy was more than anxious to go as my date.

The night of the party arrived, and immediately before leaving my house, Timi called to say that her boyfriend convinced her into going to the dinner and wanted me to pick her up. Considering Mandy was already with me, I had to tell Timi I was also bringing a date. To say it was an awkward ride is an understatement. Not only was Timi meeting her half-sister for the very first time, but she was also meeting Beth with my new girlfriend!

87

As we drove into the city, Mandy never stopped talking, making it even more uncomfortable. Arriving thirty minutes late, Carol was outside waiting for me. For the first time in 33 years, the three of us would be together. Like good old friends, the reunion with Carol was as comfortable as an old pair of slippers.

We entered the restaurant's lounge area where my guests were patiently waiting for my arrival to witness the first meeting of a daughter and her biological father. Walking in, someone yelled, "There he is." With that, Beth begins to walk toward me, and I, to her. Excitedly Beth and I hug for a long time while everyone looked on. Open-mouthed and in awe, Beth never took her eyes off me, as if meeting Santa Claus for the first time. Words weren't escaping her mouth. Finally, she was able to engage in small talk, and when she was able to regain her composure, I invited her to sing a duet with me at the piano conveniently located in the room.

Immediately after finishing our song, Mandy decided to follow Timi into the ladies' room and corner her, telling her how she wanted to be "really good friends," with her a mere three weeks after my separation! Shaken, Timi quietly turned and walked out.

After the bathroom incident, the party moved upstairs to the dining room where Beth and I sat together. It was there that I received another surprise.

Beth looked at me and says, "You know, we have a lot in common."

I responded, "Really? Like what?"

"We have the same taste in music: R&B and Gospel."

I asked, "And?"

"And we both play piano and sing."

"Okay," I replied.

With some hesitation, Beth responded, "Aaaaand, we both have the same taste in women."

"Oh — Ohhhhhhhh," slowly turning my eyes inquisitively, looking at her nodding her head up and down waiting for my reaction. As if time stood still, I realized what she was saying. To myself I thought what a coincidence that two of my three kids are gay, and then excitedly said, "Wait until you meet your brother!"

After dinner, we returned to the lounge where I sang a song I wrote for Beth called "My Little Dream," about reuniting with the daughter I hadn't seen since she was 3 days old 33 years later. For me, I was attempting to make everyone comfortable with the situation while welcoming Beth into our lives, but I failed miserably with Timi that night. She was the sunshine of my life, my best friend, but that night she felt invisible, as she later described, like a nightmare she could not awaken from. How she remained reserved and composed is a testament to her character.

Lynn would find out about the evening, every aspect of it, and immediately hired lawyers and private detectives. There was no hiding anything.

My feelings to be separated never swayed, but Lynn wanted to stay married. It didn't matter that we were both cheating. When I told her that I knew about the affair with the painter, she initially denied it until I gave her the details of how she was hiding his car.

When we talked about her cheating, I wasn't angry; I simply felt we no longer had anything. I explained how things changed, how she never returned home, and with our kids gone and my heart issues, I began to think about my own happiness and how I was living on borrowed time given my genes. What I didn't say was that I didn't want to leave this earth unhappy, never knowing real love or intimacy. But Lynn felt betrayed; she wasn't the one wanting out.

With Mandy, I was getting the attention and affection I needed, something I was missing at home no matter which home I was sleeping in. Within a short time, Timi moved out of the house, and Mandy and her young son, who had been sharing bunk beds at her parents' home, moved in. Having upgraded their lives considerably, Mandy pampered me like I was a king. Except for my relationship with Timi, I was finally happy — but that would not last long!

Unlike Timi, Damon was not having a difficult time with our divorce. Twenty-four years old, he was living the life he wanted as a gay man in the Big Apple. He had met his first real boyfriend and was keeping it relatively secret from the family. With both of us having new relationships that we weren't sharing with the world, we made plans for the four of us to have dinner in the city.

Meeting Mandy for the first time, Damon thought she was nothing more than an attractive woman without a brain, an "annoying bimbo." The only thing this meeting had in common with Timi's first meeting with her was how she spoke incessantly. Damon wishing she would "shut the fuck up," never believed I would take this relationship any further.

As time passed, the divorce got nastier and more and more expensive. New Year's Eve arrived, and I decided to buy a little cocaine to bring in the new year and forget my divorce for a night. When I took out the bag, I asked Mandy if she had ever tried it. With a look of surprise, she jumped at the chance to indulge. After partying at home with friends late into the early morning, I went to bed while Mandy stayed up all night with our guests. I awakened the following morning and found the bag of cocaine nearly empty.

Mandy, still high as was evidenced by her speech, apparently helped herself to it all night.

Lynn and I would speak occasionally, and I made every attempt to stay civil. At the beginning of our separation, Lynn had invited me to stop by her house to give her some advice about her new relationship with an old boyfriend from the Bronx. I was in town to perform as one of the duos of Don & Juan at a sold-out concert at the Hollywood Bowl – the largest audience I would ever sing for – and she knew it was an opportunity I would never pass up. We left that day on good terms, but when things did not work out between Lynn and her old boyfriend, I began to feel the wrath of a woman scorned. And you know that old saying about a woman scorned? As it turned out, no truer words were ever spoken. You could say telling the truth did not work in my favor. All I had to do was to hide my relationship with Mandy and file for divorce, stating ANY OTHER REASON than I met someone else!

Our divorce raged on, or should I say, *enraged* on.

In the end, the attorneys made out better than we did, and I would agree to terms just to be free of the marriage. Instead of just being elated I legally had my freedom and would never have to lie again, I could not remove myself from this marriage mentally until I actually became someone else's husband! So, as soon as the divorce became finalized, to my kids' dismay and disbelief, Mandy and I married in my backyard.

Partying all night, I went to bed early in the morning while Mandy stayed up through the night snorting cocaine with her sister's boyfriend. It was then I found out about an addiction problem she had with cocaine when she was younger. When I purchased the drug the very first New Year's Eve together, she never mentioned it was an issue for her in the past, and instead of declining the drug, she not only used it that night, but she had also just about finished the entire bag.

Just one month later, Timi married. Lynn and I were civil enough to walk her down the aisle together for our daughter, but I made the mistake that night of not watching over Mandy. Just like she did with Timi, she followed Lynn into the bathroom and cornered

94

her! Lynn being the passive person she was allowed Mandy to finish when Mandy added that she had hoped they would become friends! Lynn looked her boldly in the face and responded: "You will never get that home, and you will end up living in a rental!" With that, Lynn turned and walked out.

Lynn's life mission became to destroy me — at least financially if nothing else. I followed the advice of my well-paid, highly educated lawyers, and like a set of dominos, my house started crashing down all because of the attorney's recommendation to file personal bankruptcy when my former employer sued me. Little did I realize, and never could I have imagined, the problems that would result.

One by one my friends left me, some friends I had been friends with for decades. They all had one thing in common: they disliked Mandy so much they would quickly drop our friendship altogether. But I wanted the dream of the happily-ever-after to start immediately and would not slow down even when my friends advised me to do so. Being duly warned, I ignored them — and would live to regret it.

Mandy continued to overstep her bounds with everyone, and instead of achieving her goal of forming relationships, the result was always the same: people loathed her. She may have been arm candy, but beyond that she became a total embarrassment. At work, she telephoned me incessantly. If my manager told her I was busy and I'd return the call when I was done, she'd call back a minute later anyway. She called every minute on the minute until I picked up.

It was all about being happy, about being in love. I risked it all for love, for that fairytale, but, instead, I walked right into hell. I knew I made a mistake almost immediately after getting married, but I couldn't stand the humiliation of admitting this gross lack of judgment. There was no turning back. So, to keep my sanity, I did what I knew how to do best: I fooled around. That part was still easy; women were still available for one-night stands. I rarely had to pursue a woman — they pursued me. Along with that kind of lifestyle came the late-night partying and the drugs, almost as natural to me as taking my first steps.

It was not long before I was doing more and more drugs with the new friends I was meeting through Mandy, but the drugs were just as easily obtainable through my own employees, one of my salesmen, or one of my techs. Whenever we'd go out and I did not have cocaine, Mandy would enter the club and make her rounds at the bar looking for someone who did have it and flirted with them until they shared it with her.

When Mandy, whom I affectionately called "The Beast," and I weren't fighting, we were in daily pursuit of procuring cocaine. Drugs never presented a problem for me; I used them moderately and did it mostly for the camaraderie. But at my age of 60, her cocaine usage — along with my new friends she acquired for me — caused me to use more, and then the drugs became a problem for me too. My judgement became clouded, and my business began to suffer, spending less and less time at the office. If I was there, it was mainly to make collection calls or to buy drugs from one of my employees. The drugs were everywhere. As if that wasn't enough to woefully regret this marriage, I had suspicions of her infidelity.

Within a year, I was not only regretting my decision to marry Mandy, but I didn't even care about her flirting; I let someone else deal with her that night! Partying throughout the night became the norm. If we had an invitation to attend a dinner with my family, but we were with people who had blow, the blow always came first. She was never going to remove herself from them and their cocaine, and by this time, she was doing crack-cocaine.

Within two years, my life started to spiral downward when I couldn't keep up with my large alimony payments that were secured against MY home. Attempts at bank loans to fulfill my obligation to Lynn were denied due to the recent bankruptcy. Lynn and I would agree to a lower payment, but 11 months later she reneged, claiming she was not represented by an attorney, and began the proceedings to take my home too when I wasn't able to come up with the deficit for the previous 11 months plus the large alimony payments going forward. The nut was just too big to crack.

When I called to meet a friend, a wealthy real estate investor and a man who had been my best friend for decades, and offered him a deal that would benefit both of us and save my home, he saw what a mess I had become and he, too, denied me. He no longer trusted my judgment, and I was advised later that he wasn't a fan of the person **I had become** since meeting Mandy.

The more I realized that losing both homes to Lynn became more than likely, the more I used drugs to deal with the stress, eventually graduating to crack-cocaine, too. If Lynn were to win, she'd get both homes, and I would get none. Instead of starting a new life with a clean slate, my problems doubled. Both wives were attempting to get the same home! Lynn was trying to get it by suing me, and Mandy was fighting with me to have me will the house over to her so she and her son would inherit it when I died. Eighteen years her senior, she was counting on me leaving sooner than later. The more the stress piled up, the more the drugs flowed, and the worse the friends became while the respectable friends fled.

One day I was on the phone in my office when a good-looking redhead peering inquisitively walked by and then, suddenly, vanished from sight. I later found out that she was a new hire, a saleswoman. Due to the nature of the job driving to strangers' homes in the evenings and weekends, I would typically see the salespeople only once a week when they came for their paychecks and drop off new business. But this new woman, Debbie, was only in training, and it would be weeks before I'd see her again.

Debbie was hired by Richard, and I could tell immediately by the way he spoke of her that Richard was interested in having her as more than just one of his salespeople. At first glance, she was more polished than our normal salesperson and looked as if she belonged in a nice, upscale office. After meeting her, I found out that she had recently become a caregiver to her father who suffered a stroke, and her life's goal was to keep him out of a nursing home. Any 9 to 5 job wasn't working for her new lifestyle because it lacked flexibility. Like Mandy, she was Italian-American, but that is where the similarities stopped. Unlike Mandy, she was well educated, highly independent, and appeared to be very conservative.

Over the following months, I would normally see Debbie on Fridays when she came in for her paycheck and saw firsthand the problems associated with caring for her father, Ray. An affable, funny, and gregarious man, his behavior was like that of an Alzheimer's patient whereby he had no short-term memory, not two minutes, yet maintained other cognitive abilities, quick wit, and sense of humor. Ray was in constant search for his mother, a woman who had been deceased for 50 years, and, therefore, could not be left alone. In addition to his handicap, Debbie and her siblings were estranged, making life exceptionally difficult. What struck me the most was her commitment to him; he consumed her life.

One Sunday I invited Richard to come swimming at our home as he often did and said he could bring a guest. Excitedly, he accepted, and he couldn't say fast enough that he was going to invite Debbie. I knew what he thought: two couples. How wonderful was that! But it wasn't so easy even if she wanted to come. Debbie hadn't been out socially in over a year because of her father's care and cost, but Richard wanted her so badly, he arranged with the helpers and even paid them himself!! Having no work appointments and getting paid coverage for her father,

Debbie accepted the invitation. It was a beautiful hot summer afternoon, and knowing Mandy was Italian and given it was a Sunday, Debbie was expecting food. The vino flowed, but hours went by before a morsel of food was displayed. After two white wines, Debbie ended up spending her first night out in over a year on my bathroom floor! Not being a coke addict, she was expecting food!

Working late one night on collections, the phone rang. It was Debbie leaving the results of her appointments that night, and the conversation quickly turned personal. It was relatively late, and she already worked two sales jobs that day, both on the road. After a tough, miserable day, she began to tell me how people are just nuts. A coworker had just repeated a bizarre story that shocked her, but then he quickly attempted to drop the conversation, stating it was too embarrassing to repeat. I pressed her to continue, but she insisted she was too embarrassed, telling me again how surprised she was that the guy even told her. Driving and making every attempt to get off the topic, she would not respond to my questions. And then I said the magical words: "Want to stop by and smoke a joint with me?" Exhausted and feeling defeated, she said, "Do I want to smoke with you? I'll smoke with the devil tonight if he asks."

Entering the building, she walked toward my office to drop off the customers' applications, and the moment I saw her, without even uttering hello, I anxiously said, " Tell me the story." She acquiesced for two reasons: She knew I was never going to stop asking, and she knew there was a joint at the end of the story. She told me that her coworker's girlfriend, a flight attendant, let him in on what is really happening in the "friendly skies" and then went on to say that some of the male flight attendants were going into the restrooms during flights and giving each other alcohol enemas. Why alcohol this way? So, it's not detected on their breath.

In disbelief of what I was hearing coming out of her mouth, I jerked back in my chair and contemplated what she said.

Then I asked, "What do they use? Champagne?"

"Champagne?" she said laughing. Hesitating, she replied, "No, something like Vodka."

I asked, "Who would do something like that?"

To my greater disbelief, she responded, "Someone like me who doesn't like the taste of alcohol." Stunned, my eyes nearly rolled out of my head! I couldn't believe what this conservative girl was telling me.

I wanted to know exactly how this was being done. We both couldn't believe the story, and she kept commenting how we could never look at another flight attendant without wondering. At first, I dismissed it in disbelief, but she told me there are some of them that are, in fact, working under these conditions. I agreed, still somewhat inconceivable to me and kind of frightening I thought. What do you do if you're in flight and don't know if your attendant has been drinking? Do you ask to smell their ass? Are they inviting the pilots for a drink? I wanted to know how they were actually performing this, what were the logistics, as if she heard the whole story. My mind started spinning out of control.

I asked her, "Are they using tubes?"

"Tubes?" she jerked back. "Tubes? They probably have disposable enema bags," she mused. "That would make sense."

With that, I couldn't whip out a joint fast enough to ponder this story!

I could tell she was embarrassed, but I was enjoying the story too much to let it go. At that moment, my manager Richard walked in, and we all smoked a joint together. Richard asked both of us if we wanted to order something from the deli, and Debbie declined. Looking down on her lap at her paperwork, Richard left the room.

"You want an olive with that?" I asked.

She responded, "I'm not ordering anything from the deli."

I quickly replied, "No, with your **DRINK**!"

It took a moment for her to realize I was talking about the enema! Feeling mortified over the conversation, I couldn't get her attention until Richard returned.

I desperately needed help reviewing some of my out-of-control expenses and asked Debbie to take on the job, knowing she'd get it done right. Unlike most other women I've had in my life, she was self-sufficient and smart. After much coaxing, we came to an agreement that she'd work from home. Within one week, she cut these costs in half, received $10,000 in credit, and found one of my employees trying to defraud me. Our relationship, as well as my respect for her, grew.

As my life spiraled more and more out of control, I became closer to Debbie. One night at the office after all my calls were made, I asked her to share a joint with me before walking out, and we talked about the appointments and the craziness of her life. Leaving for the night, we started to separate in the parking lot walking to our respective cars when I asked her to make a bet with me, odds and evens. If she lost, she would have to come to my car window and kiss me good night. If I lost, I'd have to go to her window. Debbie was so certain that she'd win, she made the bet thinking it would amount to a peck on the cheek and she'd be free to begin her evening appointments. Not a betting woman, to her surprise, she lost. Putting her car in park, she walked over to my car and peered her head through the window. I very gently kissed her lips for a mere few seconds, and then she backed out of the window and quickly got into her car and drove away.

After that kiss, I was left wanting more. She wasn't my usual type of olive-skinned, flashy, and loose, but she quickly became my type that night. Later, when I tried to relive that kiss, she asked me to refrain from making any more advances. After all, she reminded me, I was a newlywed. Newlywed or not, the chemistry between us was undeniable. Wanting some form of closeness with her, I settled for a hug.

With Debbie being exposed to more of my business, she became increasingly concerned about the people I was associating with coming into the office and never hesitated to give me her honest opinion after having heard of my partying ways from Richard. It was her depth, honesty, and passion that endeared me to her. After a year, our relationship became physical.

Although I tried to hide my cocaine usage from her, Debbie was still suspicious and was never quiet how she felt about it either! Up until the point when Richard told Debbie that he walked in on Mandy and me doing lines of cocaine on my desk, she liked Mandy and found it hard to believe that my new wife would not only go along with me doing cocaine, but actually pushed for the whole party scene. Debbie was appalled by the way my wife cared for me, or should I say *did not* care for me, afraid I would die from my drug usage, and if I did die, she'd also be out of a job. I made every attempt to placate her over the situation, but she remained implacable. It wasn't long before we were in screaming matches either over the way the business was being run or because of my lifestyle. She was not attempting to run my life; she was trying to save it and knew I was bullshitting her. Austerely, she'd tell me how I was going to end up in jail or in a morgue if I continued to live my life that way. She greatly objected to my friends, the riffraff walking through the office, and how I was dealing with the employee she found stealing from me. She never knew that employee was supplying me drugs, but she was suspicious of why I let him off the hook so easily. I needed her help more and more but was not taking her advice. I was in too deep. When I'd flippantly or nonchalantly answer: "I only do drugs in moderation," it enraged her, and she'd lecture me like a mother, or at least someone who actually cared about me. With her temper flared up, she'd flee from the office.

Unlike the other women I became involved with, I cared about her, and I knew her scolding was coming from her heart. More than anyone else in the company or anyone I had in my life at that time except for my kids, I trusted her, and I valued her opinion. With her, I always got the truth, and she had no difficulty giving it to me straight. Shotgun straight.

Debbie and I may have had a secretive physical relationship, but it was my manager who was making every attempt to get closer to her, spending every conceivable moment Debbie would give him at her home helping with her father. Considering the estrangement with her family, she appreciated the help, and Debbie reciprocated by inviting him to join them for dinner. Richard genuinely liked and cared for both, but Debbie was never going to tolerate people believing he was more than a friend, while, at the same time, Richard was making every attempt to have everyone believe she was, in fact, HIS girlfriend. Everyone in the office knew better, and he just made a fool of himself. She may not have liked his lies about their relationship, but knowing the office knew the truth, she never made a big deal of it until she saw an enlarged photo of herself that Richard had hanging in his office. (He also had one in his bedroom!) When Debbie saw the photo in his office and heard that he told me he was expecting to move in with her within a few months because he had become essential to her, she became outraged.

After a few months of starting our affair, Debbie ended it. She knew I was not going to change, and she didn't want to be involved with a married man. But no matter how I felt about Mandy, I was not going to file for divorce considering I couldn't afford my first one. I continued to make every effort to stay friendly with Debbie because I genuinely cared about her, but being in the same room was difficult without some form of closeness. We became so estranged that she would no longer come to the office for any reason because of Mandy's constant phone calls interrupting our meetings and would only agree to meet me to go over business at a local diner if I left my cellphone in the car. I still wanted her affection, her attention; I wanted her for many reasons, but the most I was able to get was a hug as she walked out of the door.

Then one day she walked out and never returned, never even saying good-bye. I felt bad to lose an employee I valued, a real friend, but I always knew I didn't deserve her either. My life was full of disappointments, and this was just one more. But I missed her friendship, I missed her honesty, and I really missed her arms around me.

Richard never knew about my relationship with her, and even after Debbie left my employment, she remained friends with him and he continued to try and have everyone believe they were a couple, never failing to tell me when he was seeing her, thrilled he had someone like her in his life even if it was platonic. He can wish, can't he? I just remained silent and let him brag about what a great girlfriend he had!

Eventually, Richard would move in with Debbie — but not as he wished. Debbie and Ray

111

moved back to Ray's home, and Richard ended up moving into their basement as a tenant. It was a good arrangement for both until the day it wasn't.

Chapter Six

When Your Best Friend Wants to Sleep with

Your Wife

As time passed, my bitterness grew stronger each passing day. There wasn't anything someone could say to me that diminished my resentment. I was still the friendly, gregarious guy I always was to everyone around me, but I wanted to get back at the world for what the courts were doing to me, taking MY home from me. I had worked hard for decades to be able to acquire these two homes while Lynn never had to work *one* day, so I found it unfathomable I'd lose both to her. My kids would not intervene with their mother, and the lawsuit kept getting costlier. I hired an attorney in Florida to help negotiate with Lynn, and when that failed, I hired another one in New York who could not guarantee favorable results either.

Since Mandy and I fought so much when we were alone, I stayed out as much as possible. But when we were together, there were normally people around like my salesman and drug supplier, Steve, and his fiancée, but because of his fiancée's career as a physician, it was normally Steve alone. He wasn't only dealing drugs, he was involved in all kinds of shady deals, including stolen credit card information; he was the type of guy who'd sell his mother for a commission. Bad dude. We worked together years past, and he came to me looking to sell for my company. The job was straight commission, so if he was selling and not causing a problem for me with the schools or the parents, I was happy to have him. Mandy's first attraction to him was not his black skin, it was his white cocaine. It wasn't long before she'd find a "friend" in him, and he eventually became her look-out guy and report back to her what I was doing. He may have been engaged to his long-time girl, but little did I know he wanted to fuck my wife too, and he knew the way into her pants was through her nose!

The drugs took off the edge for the period of time I was high, but when they wore off, I was back to being angrier than I'd ever been in my life. For that reason, and that reason alone, I hooked up with Steve to do bad deals and started to get involved with stolen credit card information too. The three of us, Steve, Mandy, and myself, lived it up and let the credit card companies take the hit, even flying to Italy using them. Meanwhile, Steve managed to get more alone time with my wife. At this point, I wasn't jealous, but I was never going to knowingly allow a "friend" to disrespect me either. If Mandy was busy doing blow with him, it was less of her I had to deal with. I did, however, wonder about them to some extent but didn't suspect she was screwing him — foolishly thinking there was a loyalty to me, a friendship that made us "thick as thieves." It wasn't until I fell extremely ill on two separate occasions when the three of us were together that I began to suspect something sinister, something nefarious. Somehow, I was getting violently ill, giving Steve the opportunity of being alone with Mandy while I was left vomiting my guts out. The first occasion happened in Florence, Italy, and I chalked it up to food poisoning, but the odds it would happen twice when it was just the three of us was too much of a coincidence. He was a bad guy, and this

115

was something I would not put past him; I just never thought it would be ME, his best friend. I only wonder now if he had intentions of killing me but his plans fell short. And did Mandy know?

After every attempt for a bank or personal loan failed to save my home, I went to my Italian friends, "The Boys." But instead of me picking up cash from them that would pay off Lynn and end my nightmare, I got scammed! The cash turned out to be stolen checks, and when I refused to cash them, I was accused of taking two exceptionally large ones. Any one of the guys who was handling the checks could have cashed them, but I was the one they accused. Believing I owed them money, they continued to call me at the office attempting to shake me down, but I didn't have the money to meet their demands. I took their threats, hanging up on them each time, until I received a call one afternoon telling me they had seen my daughter and grandchildren on the corner that morning and "Wouldn't it be a shame if something happened to them!" That's when I caved.

It was decided I could rid myself of them and their demands if I did a "job" for them, and only then my nightmare would be over. I would get enough cash to pay Lynn off and get rid of these guys at the same time. The job consisted of "collecting" from a Mafia-connected guy who had a large gambling debt with them that he was never going to be able to pay off himself. It was never intended to be the kind of shakedown you see on TV; I was not going in to rough anyone up. Actually, I wasn't going in at all. There would be a few big, threatening-looking guys to frighten them. That would be the extent of the shakedown — just enough to scare them into handing over his cash. I'd go to my employee Mike, my other drug supplier, to supply the guys; they were no one I knew.

My Mafia contact and the man we were collecting from had been friends in the past but subsequently became bitter enemies. Because of their former friendship, my contact also knew his CPA, another gambling associate, and knew about his client's safe with cash and jewels. I never knew the whole story or how much of it was true, but I wanted

117

to be free of them and didn't care about the particulars. I was instructed to go to the CPA's office and get the new address of his client who had likely relocated in the hopes of not being found by his nemesis. As instructed, I went to the CPA's office with Michael and his guys, and out of fear upon seeing Mike's brutes, the CPA agreed to drive me to his client's home while Michael's guys followed.

To my surprise, the robbers went in with a gun. That was never the plan as I knew. The robbery would likely not have been a problem had the man's wife not arrived home early. Mike's guys pulled out a gun, telling him to open his safe, and then tied him and his wife up. The robbers got away with some cash and jewels, but not what we were expecting, and not nearly enough to pay Lynn off.

After all that, I lost my home anyway! Devastated, Mandy and I moved into a rental just five houses away from her dysfunctional family — just as my first wife promised she would!

In typical Mandy style, she came to me complaining she was overdrawn on her checking account. Handing me the statement, she requested that I take over the account knowing I'd replenish any deficits. Each month thereafter she handed me her statement without viewing it. Within only a month after losing my home and moving to New Jersey, instead of her statement showing a minimal amount at month's end, there was suddenly $200,000 deposited into it. The bank had erroneously added three zeros to her deposit! Had this happened a few months prior, I would have paid Lynn off with it.

Feeling desperate and bitter over the courts taking my home, I had no intentions of being magnanimous by returning the money and began to withdraw the money in $9900 increments, never disclosing to Mandy what had happened.

I was in the office one day when Steve walked in and told me he heard about the robbery I did with Michael. His cockiness made him feel insulted that he wasn't told, as if he was the Godfather or something. I was getting more suspicious of him with Mandy, so I devised a plan. Together, Steve and I flew to Florida, and on the day we were both scheduled to return home, I told him to go alone as I needed more time at the Florida office. To no one's knowledge, I flew back that evening to come home and find my house empty. When Mandy walked through the door at 2 a.m., I knew what she was doing and who she was doing it with. Lying who she was with, I was going to call them until she confessed that she was in fact with Steve.

The following day I called Steve to tell him he was never to go near my wife again. I left and stayed in New York City for a week. Steve wasn't going to fight me; he wasn't going to break up his new marriage with a physician and give up that gig for Mandy, just a white chick with a cocaine habit. The pleasure was in fucking me! We parted ways professionally and personally. He was jealous of me, and the best way to knock me down was by literally fucking my wife.

Michael was let go shortly thereafter.

Mandy knew everything I was doing, and I was trapped. If I didn't tell her, Steve had. There wasn't anything she could say that I could believe. She lied so much that she believed her own lies. I didn't trust anything about her. Absolutely nothing.

It wasn't long before the Feds started to come around and question me. Steve had been arrested on his credit card fraud, and to negotiate a lesser sentence, he gave them MY crime! You could say it was his parting gift to me.

Knowing my arrest was eminent, I took Timi and Damon to lunch and broke the news that I was in trouble. Stunned, they accepted the information and left more confused than when they arrived but not surprised given how much I had changed. I lost nearly every friend and relative I had. All I knew was I made the biggest mistake of my life by divorcing Lynn knowing we could have remained living apart and lived separate lives. But that illusion of love was more than any drug, more dangerous, more costly than I ever imagined. It makes you lose your senses; it makes you lose your mind. And when love falls short, is it lack of substance or were my expectations too high? I

121

wanted love; Mandy wanted cocaine. I could have gotten past her complete ignorance to all matters in general had she kept her mouth shut, but that loquacious bitch always chose to speak and embarrass me.

Before my one-year anniversary at the new apartment, I was sitting in my cardiologist's chair waiting to have a medical test performed when I answered my cellphone. It was Mandy's sister telling me the Feds came to arrest me. I quickly pulled off the electrodes stuck to my body and left surreptitiously. As I exited the building, the Feds were there to receive me.

122

Chapter Seven

The Real Cost of Living My Dream

I was just about to turn 64 in a few days, and instead of planning a party for the occasion, the Feds had other plans by escorting me to the White Plains courthouse to be processed for burglary — with a gun. Despite all of this, I wasn't overly concerned. After being visited by the FBI months ago, I had hired an attorney, using the money our bank inadvertently deposited into Mandy's account, and felt this whole situation would be short-lived, as I was not at the scene of the crime, never saw a gun, requested one, and, therefore, I wasn't nearly as involved as Mike's boys. I would soon be advised that I could not have been more wrong!

My attorney met me at the jailhouse the day I was arrested to brief me on what to expect before the judge that same day. I was expecting the judge to set bail and I'd go back to my life, this time with the added stress of getting out of this nightmare. The absolute most I was expecting was a few months behind bars. But the judge saw it quite differently. The prosecutor argued vehemently against any bail, claiming that not only was I a flight risk, but I was, in fact, the leader in this crime, declaring I was the educated businessman who set up and executed the plan, and my group who did commit the crime were just my uneducated, criminal flunkies. The prosecutor's valiant argument rendered me three weeks in jail before my next hearing to argue bail once again.

From there, I was taken to the jailhouse in Valhalla, New York. Not only was it just blocks from Hawthorne where I attended reformatory school, but it was the very same jail the administrators at Hawthorne used to tell me I'd end up! Unlike the FBI who treated me fairly when arresting me, these cops made sure to express their passive aggressive ill feelings toward me by blaring rap music on the car radio. Just the day before, no one would have treated me this way. No one!

After being processed, I was assigned to a cell block that consisted of three floors, housing approximately 100 men, each inmate with their own cell. The block had one L-shaped communal area where we ate and watched television. The first day out in the yard I knew without speaking to any of them that these men were hardened criminals, real street guys. You just knew it. I didn't belong there. Whenever someone approached me to start a conversation, they always opened with the same question: "What are you in for?" I would answer laconically, not being my gregarious self. Why would I be? I wasn't looking to make friends or enemies; I was getting out soon.

In the few conversations I had with Mandy, she wasn't concerned about me or my predicament; she was more worried about herself and how she was going to pay her bills. But what she was most concerned about was how she was going to finance her coke habit. She didn't care as much about paying the rent because she knew she could easily go live five doors down with her parents again even though they absolutely didn't want her. I didn't have to ask her father's permission to marry her – he asked *me* to marry her so that he didn't have to deal with her anymore!

As the weeks passed, the state of my involvement was getting more real, or should I say, *sur*real. Even when my attorney visited, we spoke through a glass window, making me feel more like a "lifer," — someone too dangerous to be in the same room with humans. After a while, I started to play basketball in the yard to keep my sanity. I wasn't assigned any job because of my age, and the hours just dragged. I called Timi every day, racking up a $1,500 a month phone bill! She was the only one I trusted, and she was the one communicating with my attorney. Mandy was never even a consideration, especially with something so serious. After everything we had been through, Timi was still willing to do anything for me. And the jail never made anything easy.

If I needed something, it had to come from the commissary or directly from the manufacturer in their packaging. I needed my reading glasses that were left in my car when I was arrested, but the jail would not allow anyone to deliver them to me. I had to wait for the manufacturer to mail a pair, leaving me unable to even read for a month.

In the beginning, I would call my office a few times a week and give directions to my bookkeeper Jim to send money to my commissary, how to handle any matters that arose at the office and, except for me working on collecting my receivables, the office ran much the same. But that would not last long either.

Because of the lawsuit with my former employer, I wanted to secure my receivables and began to operate my business under Richard's company the year before. Richard knew nothing about running a business, and the only asset he had was a business name. Fortunately, that was all I needed to keep my business and the income out of my name while Lynn was still fighting me. So shortly after I was arrested and it became apparent I was not returning soon, Jim stopped accepting my collect calls. Instead, he had developed a relationship with Mandy in the hopes it would lead to an affair. Jim was married for nearly 25 years, but he wanted to sleep with my wife. He succeeded in seducing her, spending as much time with her as she allowed, and his wife threw him out.

127

Not a good-looking man and nearly toothless, he fell for Mandy's flirting believing it was actually genuine. But Mandy knew he had my checkbook and was willing to prostitute herself for it. This enabled her to keep the apartment and keep her comfortable in the lifestyle I had gotten her accustomed to. She may have still been sleeping with Steve, but because of his recent marriage, he was not going to be supplying her coke free of charge on a regular basis.

When Jim stopped taking my calls, my son Damon went to the office to speak to him and said that I needed access to my business. Mandy was working part-time for my company merely answering the phones when she was in the mood or didn't have a nail or hair appointment, and when she saw Damon, she became indignant, stating that she was now the rightful owner of the business, she and Jim were running it, and I had nothing to do with it any longer. Unlike Timi, Damon had stayed neutral about Mandy, thinking she was harmless until that moment. After blasting Damon, she snapped at Jim demanding they go to the bank immediately and withdraw everything she could. When there was no more money coming into the business and Jim could no longer afford Mandy's bills, she left him. Jim ended up living with his brother, and, as expected, Mandy lost the apartment.

One day, when visiting with the inmate in the adjacent cell to mine, he told me how he was able to talk to the female prisoner who was housed directly above him by inserting a hollow tube similar to the one you'd find in the middle of a roll of paper towels into his toilet bowl and extending it into the bowl's trap. I didn't believe him until he proved it to me. While there, he called her from the toilet bowl, and the conversation quickly became sexual. He never disclosed I was there, and it probably would not have mattered to her as I clearly heard her moaning while masturbating. It was the prisoner's version of telephone sex.

In my cell one day, a female guard handed me a handwritten note from a female prisoner in the building across from me, approximately 150 feet away. She saw me playing basketball from her window and described me to the guard. We soon became pen pals, and that, too, became sexual rather quickly, asking me which position I preferred during sex, etc. She never became vulgar because she knew the notes were likely being read by the guards. She told me how one day she was able to see me from my unit's window at night. From that distance, I was barely able to see her, but just the fact of having a female friend there meant something to me. One day her note instructed me to go to my window at 8 p.m. where I would see her, and she'd flash me. Excitedly, at 8 p.m., I went to the window in my block and watched her strip from the waist up. Regardless of the strange situation, she made me feel somewhat special — that is, until I found out that she was baring her breasts for two other floors! She wanted me to show her MY package, but I was not going to flash her in front of all the guys in my cell block. Our relationship continued for four months until she was either released or moved to another prison. All I know, she went dark.

The inmate in the other adjacent cell to me was a Black man I became very friendly with. We always had each other's back. One day at breakfast, a Spanish inmate began arguing with him over the use of the microwave.

Not wanting to get the guards' attention, they agreed to meet in the yard to battle it out. My Black friend was there to fight with his hands, but the Spanish inmate thought it wise to bring a weapon and stabbed my friend with a shiv — a toothbrush filed to a sharp point with a string wrapped around one end to form a handle that was considered contraband and highly punishable if caught with one. When the fight broke out, I witnessed that no matter who your friends were, the Spanish stayed with the Spanish and the Blacks stayed with the Blacks. All prior friendships were meaningless. I had sung with minorities, lived with them, played basketball with them, and above all thought we were all brothers until that day when racism came to the yard.

I was in prison just a few months when the bank discovered their mistake. By this time, I had spent $110,000 of it. Mandy had apparently opened her statement and saw the balance the month after I was arrested and when she questioned me, I told her the truth. Since I had been away and lost control over my account, she tried to withdraw more than $9,900, flagging it at the bank.

I was put into protective custody three months after arriving, which meant I was not with the general population because I had been seen talking to one of the other defendants in my case in the yard one day, and the Feds didn't like the assumed collaboration, so they made sure we were kept separated. At the next meeting with my attorney, I was informed that the Mafia head, who ordered the robbery I was involved in, was murdered. I could only assume it was his rival, the man we robbed, who ordered the hit. With him dead, that left me as one of the two top men associated with the burglary, thereby giving me the most time to serve.

In protective custody, there were approximately 40 men, each with their own cells, and only allowed into the yard for one hour each day. Being locked up with the hardest of criminals, I kept to myself as much as possible, but the environment was unnerving, to say the least, which was exactly what the Feds wanted in the hopes of breaking me and giving up my accomplices. They were after the big guys I had met, but I was never going to talk, especially after the murder. I was always going to protect my kids no matter what the cost to me.

To pass the time, I played chess in my cell. My opponent was either another inmate who was assigned chores in the unit and had time before they had to report back to their own cell, or I placed the chessboard on the floor outside of my cell and played with the man in the adjacent cell. Uncomfortable as it was, we twisted our bodies to see the moves.

In protective custody, there was never a silent moment, not even during the long nights — enough to make nearly anyone break. But I remained strong and silent. Steve may have given me up to reduce a crime he committed unassociated with me, but I was never going to involve anyone. Steve was jealous I had operated a good business up until the time I got involved with him and Mandy's crowd, and I'm sure part of it was planned so he could have time with my wife while I was away. I had gotten myself in this mess; I was going to pay my own dues and never be a snitch regardless. I dealt with the devil and got burnt. What a surprise!

I had been advised by my attorney to proffer so I could make a deal and receive considerably less time. I was still not going to talk about anyone other than myself, and the only caveat was there could be no lies. If it was discovered anything given was not truthful, the deal was void. The biggest obstacle was the gun charge that carried the bulk of the time. He insisted I proffer that I knew about the gun on the morning of the crime. When I objected, he insisted the prosecutor's office had evidence from the other parties involved that I did, in fact, know about it, and, therefore, they were not going to believe my version of the story. My "flunkies" set me up to make a deal for themselves, and they all received much less time than I did. Believing my attorney knew better than I did, I ever so begrudgingly took his advice.

I was questioned nonstop for two days, not only about the crime, but also about the fraudulent credit cards. When questioned if I had used any of my clients' information to obtain these cards, I truthfully answered no. But unbeknownst to me, Steve was taking MY clients' information from their credit applications, duplicating credit cards, and blaming it on me. The government didn't believe me, so the deal to be released early was off.

One day the guards escorted me into a private visiting room where my attorney was waiting, a glass divider separating us. My lawyer immediately informed me not to be seated; I didn't even get the obligatory hello because he was in too much of a rush and pushed the documents through a small slit under the glass, stating it explained the deal being offered. I anxiously asked him what it said, and he replied that it was best to read the entire offer on my own. When pressed, he merely insisted he had to leave. Fraught with anxiety, the walk back to the cell felt like miles. As the familiar loud clang of steel bars shut behind me and I heard the dangling and clinging of the keys locking me in, my index finger had already ripped open the large envelope. As my eyes came into focus, I stood there frozen: 12 years!

Like the disbelief of losing a loved one, my mind went into shock over losing my own life. I would be 74 when released with good behavior, if I lived that long, and my mind was spinning as I sunk deeper into despair, never believing what was in front of me. All I could think of was how my life was over, so I began to contemplate suicide. I studied the room and decided how I was going to rip my sheets, wrap them around a pipe on the ceiling, and then tie them around my neck. I would step on the chair and kick it from under me, leaving me dangling for minutes before succumbing to death. But the thought of putting my kids and grandkids through that became unthinkable.

Twelve years was nothing like what we had discussed, and it explained why my attorney requested a room with glass between us. Like a frightened rat, he ran. He became disillusioned with me when he discovered I used the bank's money to pay him and began to treat me poorly. Disillusioned as he was, he never returned the unused portion of the retainer he took from me, nor did he return it to the bank.

I immediately fired him, and Timi borrowed money from a friend to hire a high-profile, highly arrogant attorney, telling me he was not going to be holding my hand through this ordeal. I didn't need his hand; I needed to get out of jail! But the first thing he did do was get me released from protective custody.

He felt he could get me a reduced sentence for time served until he read what I proffered. Had I not stated I had known about the gun that morning, he felt he could have gotten that charge dropped completely, but there was no turning back. Had I then gone back and said I lied because my attorney advised me to do so, there was nothing the prosecutor would have believed from me.

The Feds kept me in protective custody for a total of six months, and when I was returned to the general population, I was left with eye problems, likely from the loss of light, that would remain with me to this day. And when my new attorney went before the judge to fight the gun charge, the judge postponed the trial, setting the next date for another year away!

Who should I have blamed? It was easier if I blamed it all on someone else, but ultimately, it was me. They were all my decisions except for one, a brandished gun, and that was the one that carried a seven-year term alone. It only took one. The FBI said: "I enjoyed the lifestyle," and that's true, but I'd never hurt anyone for it. It was my bitterness toward the courts for losing my two homes, and for sticking it to the big credit card companies, I just didn't care. I got screwed, so why not them too.

Once out of protective custody, I met a new fellow inmate named Steve, also of Jewish descent, and we quickly became friends, attending all Jewish services together. Steve was a middle-aged man who had worked for the school system as a principal and was married to an assistant superintendent of schools. Having lived a nice, respectable, middle-class life, he was having a difficult time dealing with his imprisonment, and I liked having someone I could help assimilate into this hell. I could never understand why he couldn't be released on bail for a white-collar crime like tax evasion, but it would be years before I would discover the shocking truth.

Throughout the entire time, other than the day I was arrested and appeared before the judge, Mandy had only visited me once! Every phone call made to her was converted to her needs. Although a healthy woman, she had no intentions of getting a normal job. It was easier to seduce a man who wouldn't ordinarily have the opportunity of sleeping with an attractive woman and get them to pay her bills.

It was approaching two years of my incarceration when I phoned one of my salesmen, Doug. A long-time friend as well, Doug and I talked about business and followed up with our favorite topic: Richard. It was always a joke how he pined for Debbie and got nowhere and the fact he was living in Debbie's basement. The gossip-loving character he was, Doug called Debbie to see how things were with Richard living there and wanted to know if he was paying his rent. Richard was still placing schools, but liquor came first to him the older he became. As Richard's favorite subject, my name came up. Knowing Debbie had been a good friend and someone who was sympathetic to my situation, Doug suggested I write to her. Not only could Doug give me her address, but he further tells me that after eight years of caring for her father, he had recently passed, and as far as Doug knew, she was unattached.

Merely a year after our affair ended, my life really started to spiral out of control, and I would end up living like a caged animal. In bed at night, I would rewrite the past in my mind where my ex-wife, my new wife, and I all become good friends, and everyone is happy — or they become happy. There's always a happy ending, but the ending in my head was so much better than outside of it. I obsessed over the millions of dollars in receivables I lost — over the life I lost. I had lost everything, no assets whatsoever to leave my kids or for myself. I always knew I could survive prison because of my childhood, but it was not me. I didn't belong there, never did. I didn't know how I would start my life over in my 70s.

Feeling aggrieved, I think of this precipitous fall from heaven and how blind I was all because I wanted my fairytale to begin right away when I could have maintained the same existence with my first wife while she could have continued to do whatever she was doing with whatever worker while I could have done the same up north. But, instead, I passionately pursued this new idyllic life with a much younger wife that ultimately left me living yet another lie — and with much less money.

Every morning my first year I woke up believing I'd be free before long and I'd return to my business as usual and could deliver some explanation to the employees that they would be only too happy to accept. It would be like Moses returning to his flock. No fanfare.

I hadn't thought about Debbie in some time, especially after our bitter ending that I cared to forget, but after Doug suggested I contact her, I thought about the good times we had together. But more importantly, I remembered her character. Having been locked up for two years, I was already thinking about the people left in my life — the ones that mattered other than my kids. There were so few and nearly none I could count on for anything anymore. Mandy was nothing more than a colossal mistake, and I had already lost the friends I had before marrying her. If one of my friends wanted to remain in my life, it was their wife that objected fiercely. I also knew that had I taken my friends advice and not married Mandy, I never would have been in this situation. I had only myself to blame.

Within two days, I had constructed a letter to Debbie and mailed it. I had no expectations. It had been nearly five years since we had last seen each other. Her departure was not exactly a civil one, no good-bye, no text, no nothing. She was right about the

141

things that made her angry with the business; it affected her little income as it was, and I knew it, but I couldn't change Richard from lying about appointments. I couldn't even change myself. Until one day, Uncle Sam changed it for me.

Debbie was living in a beautiful condo when we met, and she had recently taken in her father and became his caregiver. Her life was incredibly hard because of her father's handicap, and to make it even more difficult, Richard was always bullshitting her about new leads and appointments week after week. I couldn't help but feel sorry for her, and I genuinely liked her father, an affable, retired bookie from Jersey City who loved to talk! I gained a lot of respect for her almost immediately, and time would show her true intelligence and tenacity.

If Debbie didn't respond to my letter after being incarcerated for two years, after opening up to her, I was ready to accept it. I had been through so much; that disappointment was not going to kill me. But I had hoped she would. She was one of the most honest and honorable people I knew, smart, and to have her as my friend again would be nothing less than a blessing. She only spoke the truth to me, something I wasn't used to. And she had a real Italian temper that went off like a firecracker. She meant business. But she was soft too, especially with her father and the customers. But what I remembered most clearly was her yelling at Richard because he was always trying to bullshit her, and it never went well for him.

Each day at mail call I waited with anticipation wondering if she'd even bother to answer me. Receiving mail was monumental; it was my only link to the outside world other than the people who were on my calling list, which weren't many due to the high cost and limitations of phone usage. A few people wrote, but that fell off quickly. When I was first arrested, I had the bank's money and used it freely for commissary, but when the bank discovered their mistake, they quickly took back the remaining $90,000, leaving me with nothing. Not only was Mandy not helping me, but she then had to hire an attorney for herself for the issue with the bank and had to borrow the money from her family for her defense.

I relied on Timi for everything, wearing her to a shadow and affecting her marriage. If Debbie came back into my life, I would have someone else to lean on, someone to emotionally support me. I needed her. All I had was hope.

A week passed by even more slowly than the week prior before I finally heard my name during mail call. I knew it could be anything: a letter from my attorney, a note or card from any one of my long-lost friends, but I had hoped it was from the one person I needed. Jumping to grab it, my heart beating faster, I stood there frozen for a moment until I was able to read the name on the envelope. It was her.

Walking back to my cell to open it felt like miles, but I needed to read it sitting down in my own quietude. I didn't know what to expect. Was I opening myself up to her wrath? That seemed more than plausible knowing how angry she could get. Considering the way she left five years prior, I had no reason to believe she would even be kind to me.

Without any hesitation in her writing, I was elated to see my fears were unfounded, and the kind-hearted woman I had known was there again. She didn't scold me for the past, but expressed her feelings

144

not only about me, but her loathing for Mandy, holding back nothing. I wasn't offended; she was right. But she also wrote how sympathetic she was to my situation regardless, having known my character by the way I took care of my customers and my staff, the "straight" employees, helping my customers and salespeople when they needed a loan even when my own cash was low.

I immediately wrote back and asked for her phone number. I wanted to speak to her again, to hear her voice, to have that friend back I so needed, but when she responded, she omitted her phone number or any mention of speaking to each other. After two attempts and receiving no number, I asked her to call my daughter Timi who would testify I was a changed man, no more bullshit, no more lies. She didn't respond to that either, but her letters continued.

It was December of 2005, already incarcerated for over two years, and I still had no trial date. The hardest part was the not knowing. My kids were beyond tired of my situation and seldom visited. At least Timi was always available on the phone and took care of my needs as they arose. Like a child who needs their mother to survive, I needed her.

Then, one day, Timi told me a friend was coming to the prison to see me on Christmas morning. The only reason to even tell me was to ensure I would shave and look the best I possibly could. Plus, I'd have something to look forward to if nothing else. When I asked who it was, Timi just said the person wanted to surprise me. In my mind, I dismissed that it could be Debbie, telling myself an Italian girl wasn't coming here on Christmas morning. It had to be another Jew.

Christmas morning arrived, and a guard came to my cell to escort me into the family visiting room. Walking into the large, noisy visiting room, every table filled with visitors, inmates, and guards, I looked around, not knowing who I was looking for amongst the 50 or so tables. But it took only seconds to see Debbie's red hair, and I sprinted to get to her 30 feet away. It felt like miles.

Nearly five years had passed since we had last seen or spoken to each other and more than eight years since we had first met. We looked different, both older, I, a bit thinner, and she, a bit heavier. I was apprehensive approaching her, but then she stood up, arms extended. I had been so deprived of human touch except for the demeaning and violating cavity searches, I didn't want to let go, but this hell had restrictions on that too: 10 seconds. Not only were we limited to the time we could hug or kiss, but it was only allowed when I first entered the room and when we parted. In between, we had to sit across the table from each other, not side-by-side, only allowed to hold hands above the table.

Before entering the room, Debbie had to wait her turn to get into the visiting room, and then once inside, she waited another 20 minutes for me to be called and escorted in. Not knowing what to expect, the time waiting was stressful for her. Fortunately, Timi had warned her how to dress or she'd be turned away after making the hour-long drive. No metal on the clothing. If the detector caught it, you were turned away. This meant she could not wear an underwire bra or jeans with a metal button, and sleeveless or see-through tops were thought to be too provocative and, therefore, prohibited to enter the visitors' room.

Her level of discomfort was so palpable, so much so that one of the female guards came over and asked if this was her first visit. She responded by telling her that it was her first visit to *any* prison. The guard thanked her for coming, telling her how important it was to prisoners to receive visitors. Ironically, this guard was one of the toughest ones we had and thought to be cold hearted, so her attempt at making Debbie comfortable and welcome was very much a surprise. Maybe she was interested in Debbie!?

At exactly one hour later a guard approached and informed us that our hour was up. But before leaving, I ask Debbie if she would return the following week on New Year's Eve. I tried to express what the holiday meant to me growing up, as it represented facing another year without my father, many years without any family at all. It wouldn't be until I was married with my own children that I began to love and celebrate that night. But once behind bars, I was thrown back into despair on that night. Even with that, Debbie was noncommittal about returning. Standing to say good-bye, we kissed — not a long, passionate kiss, but a kiss nevertheless; my first kiss in two years.

I wanted to grab her the way I did in the past, to feel her skin, to take in every breath, but I knew I would be thrown into the hole had I done that. For one moment I felt human again, until I walked out of the room and had to endure another humiliating cavity search to see if Debbie had passed me drugs.

Debbie gave me her phone number, and it was planned to call her on Wednesday nights. Only once a week because of the cost. That Wednesday I asked her again to visit me that weekend for New Year's Eve. Feeling sorry for me, she acquiesced to visit before driving to Atlantic City, the opposite direction, to spend the holiday with her cousins.

Saturday night arrived, and it felt like date night as I prepared for our first date by shaving. Because it was an evening visit, Debbie waited on a line outside in the freezing cold to just get into the building before being inspected herself, even inspecting her mouth for drugs. Not only did they check everyone's mouth, but they checked the babies' diapers for the same.

When I entered the visiting room, I immediately saw Debbie sitting at the far end of the room. When she saw me, she stood up against the back wall and waited for me to approach, not extending her arms. Nearly skipping to her, the anticipation was almost overwhelming. Stopping two feet before her, she stared into my eyes and merely said, "Kiss me." My heart skipped a beat or two, and for one moment, we were eight years younger as we were wrapped in each other's arms again. Breaking apart after 10 seconds was unnatural and cruel.

At our assigned table, no one behind us, it felt almost private, practically romantic. All we needed was a candle. We didn't need drinks; we didn't need food; we only needed to hold each other's hands, and we never let go for one full hour. It was then I asked her to stay in my life and not just as a pen pal.

But this time things were **considerably** different. She explained that the reason she came to visit me the week before was for her own benefit; she needed to see how she felt after five years. She had gotten over me, never even inquiring about me, but living with Richard in the same house guaranteed she'd never forget me with all his stories about my arrest. He was actually jovial about it. She never disclosed to Richard that I contacted her, nor did she tell him she was visiting. She didn't want to hear his resentment. Even from prison, I managed to take the woman he wanted. He may have wanted her, feeling he was getting closer to moving onto the floor she occupied, but that was never going to happen. She had remained friends with him, always appreciating his care and help with her father, but it would never go any further.

Somehow, I had gotten back into her heart, but I didn't know how deep. I explained that I wanted her in my life as my girlfriend, and she made it clear that was not going to happen if I remained married; she was not going to play this game with me again. Without hesitation, I wanted her back in my life and welcomed the thought of filing for a divorce from Mandy. I had nothing to lose except Mandy herself, and I'd gain the best friend I could ever need.

Debbie expressed her concern for not knowing the amount of time I'd be away and what her family would think. She wasn't going to lie to anyone — even about me. I told her I expected to be out in a year or so. Debbie had hoped I had the courage to leave Mandy years ago and live a clean life together with the years I had left, but I chose to remain married because I couldn't afford a second divorce. I couldn't even afford my first one. I told her then I needed $2,000,000 to get me out of my financial hole. During one of our epic arguments before leaving my employment, she told me in anger that if she had $2,000,000, she'd pay someone to take me out with it, but she'd have to borrow the $2,000,000 from me! I'd finance my own hit.

Debbie continued to visit me on Sunday mornings without Richard knowing — or so we thought.

With Debbie's help, I immediately started divorce proceedings, but by the time we were able to get the correct forms and have them notarized, Mandy's divorce papers were delivered to me. She beat me to the punch by mere days! She waited the minimum 10-year mark to be able to collect social security from me, and then filed the divorce papers. Once Debbie came into my life, I had no reason to call or answer Mandy. She was insulted I wouldn't answer her letters and proceeded to file for divorce, thinking I'd be devastated. She had hoped. But she was dead wrong.

In a letter to Debbie shortly thereafter, I opened up about everything, especially our past. There wasn't a single personal thing between us that I failed to mention. I wanted her to know that I hadn't forgotten anything we shared; it all meant something. I was anxious for her to receive the letter and know how it affected her — how it was going to affect *us*. But weeks went by, and every time I asked, she said it never arrived. By then, I insisted it was Richard who took it, but she was convinced it was just lost in the mail. She was certain Richard would never steal her mail.

A week went by, and after returning home from work one Friday night, Debbie entered her home to find a note from Richard on the kitchen table saying he was arrested for back child support dating back years. Richard's kids were both adults, but when he opened a bank account after moving to Debbie's home, it was flagged, and the police picked him up.

153

Searching for something in her basement, Debbie finds MY LETTER! Richard took it out of the mailbox, opened it, read it, and decided to keep it. In disbelief, Debbie became infuriated, and when Richard tried calling her from the jailhouse the same day, she laced into him so badly she thought he would be disemboweled through the phone. All she could hear through her own screams were, "But...but.... but.... but" before slamming the phone down. Richard continued to call that same day, each time having to listen to her wrath and never getting a word in. She then blocked the jail's phone number. Once he was released weeks later, he had to have the police call to inform her he was picking up his belongings. It would be years before they would speak again.

Her letters continued each week. And instead of getting a letter every day or two, she'd write a 15-page story to me. As soon as I received it, I returned to my cell, poured myself hot water and made a cup of coffee while I devoured every word. They were about her family, her troubles, but she wrote much of her time and adventures in Italy beginning decades past. I loved every story; it was a lifeline. She had so much to tell me.

While waiting in line one day when visiting me, Debbie began a conversation with the woman in front of her, Mary, who happened to be the wife of my fellow inmate and friend, Steve. Having heard me speak of him, Debbie immediately made the connection. Debbie talked about the cost of the collect phone calls from me, and Mary explained that she purchased a cellphone with a local phone number to the prison and, therefore, had minimal phone charges. They exchanged phone numbers, so Mary could provide Debbie with the information on how to get a phone, which then allowed us to speak every day.

I had told Debbie from the beginning that I was expecting to be released in another year or so, but it took another 10 months after I said that when my case would even get to trial. Until that time, the extent of my involvement hadn't become real until the moment the judge dropped the gavel: 10 years, a mere 2 years less than the original offer. Merely 2 years! It was then that it became all too real.

My concern was not only if I'd get out alive, but now that there was more than six years left before I was scheduled to be released on good behavior, far more than I expected and far more than I asked Debbie to wait for me. I didn't know if she'd run. She was 14 years my junior, still nice looking, and she didn't need me or my baggage. She wouldn't come to the courthouse; it was more than she could deal with, so I didn't know what to expect when I phoned her to explain. As anxious as I was to speak to her and ask that all-too-important question "Will you wait for me?" she assured me she would, but I always knew there was a chance she could say good-bye on any call, and each week I continued to ask if she was still waiting, asking "Are you keeping the porch light on for me?"

After my sentencing, I was sent to a federal prison at Fort Dix in New Jersey. Even though Fort Dix was in the same state as Debbie, it was double the distance compared to Valhalla for her, and the visits every Sunday morning dwindled to once every month or two. It was the same exercise in futility before allowing her into the visitors' room. Unlike Valhalla, this room was double the size and had rows of uncomfortable, attached chairs with no tables. They also had vending machines, but the inmates themselves were not allowed to approach them; it was strictly for the guests. Sitting next to each other, our contact was still limited and hands always visible. One day while sitting next to another inmate I knew and his wife, the four of us carried on a conversation when a guard came over to put an end to it. I was threatened twice that they'd abruptly end my visit.

Fort Dix had three different sections divided by the severity of the crime. Not qualifying for the low group with the most freedom because of my gun charge, I was placed in the middle group with approximately 800 inmates, the largest of the three. Instead of being confined to a single cell like I had in county jail, we had 25-30 prisoners in each room, all sleeping in bunk beds. Fortunately, I was able to get assigned a bottom bunk from the first day due to my age.

After being assigned a bunk, I walked directly to the gym to check it out and noticed a big, muscular Muslim man bench pressing. He started with 200 lbs., increased to 300, which got everyone's attention, and then added another 100 lbs.! With that, he went to pick up yet another 100 lbs. of weights to add, now 500 lbs., then paused and looked around, and said, "Hey, I'm just fuckin' with you." Everyone laughed. I immediately liked him.

Returning to my room, I found my new bunkie turned out to be the same Muslim guy from the gym. We immediately hugged and remained friends until he was sent to another prison months later.

Not only did I have more freedom in this federal prison compared to county, but this facility offered more activities, a gym, and email! A prisoner count was done each morning before breakfast and then after dinner, but other than that, we were free to go between our room and the gym. Once I arrived at Fort Dix, I quickly met men who had similar interests in music, and together we formed a singing group, performing mostly oldies. We sang for all the church services, memorials, and most holiday events in the yard, drawing the largest crowds of any event. The other prisoners loved our harmony, and the singing and the group kept me sane. Performing for the other inmates, I could forget where I was and enjoyed it just as much as I did for any audience as a free man.

My singing group was called into the priest's office one day regarding the mass that weekend, Easter Sunday. After assembling, the priest announces to us that we could not sing for mass that Sunday, Easter Sunday, because "One of us did not have Christ in his heart." He had just found out that I was Jewish and didn't appreciate me singing for his congregation.

"I guess that would be me," I quickly responded. "I don't understand!"

"How would you like it if I sang at your temple? the priest retorted.

"If you sang our songs, that would be okay," I said.

The priest hesitated before asking me to leave for 10 minutes so that he could speak to the other singers privately. During those minutes, I stewed. We had been practicing *The Lord's Prayer* for two months — and we sounded good!

Upon returning to the group, the priest explained that after speaking with the others and considering the song to be performed was *The Lord's Prayer*, in particular, the answer was still no. I couldn't sing!

I immediately replied, "Father, if Jesus Christ wanted to sing in your church, you wouldn't allow Him? Like me, He was born a Jew, and He died a Jew."

The priest paused for 10 seconds, his head hanging, but it felt more like hours, knowing I could be put into the hole for going back at him. The others knew it too. Finally, he lifted his head, looked at the guys, then me, and said: "See ya all on Sunday."

After that, I never had an issue singing for any occasion.

Timi came to visit one Sunday with two of my three grandchildren but were turned away because the kids weren't dressed to code. In the limited time frame given for visitors, Timi had to find a clothing store, purchase the appropriate garments, and then return to

160

the prison before going through inspection again. My youngest grandchild, Cole, was a baby when I was arrested and had been told I was in the Army to explain why he hadn't seen me. As I entered the visitors' room, my grandchildren came running toward me, screaming, "Grandpa, Grandpa, Grandpa," so loudly that everyone in the room turned to see what the commotion was about. My heart went to my throat. It had been over two years since I had seen them. Because they were both so young, the guards did and said nothing. The kids obtained food from the vending machines, and five-year-old Cole complained to his mother about the food the Army was serving their men.

Passing through the communal room one day, I was hit from behind in the head by a Muslim named Mohammed. I was hit so hard I blacked out. I knew the guy and we were never friendly. He didn't like the fact that I would walk into the communal room to pick up a chessboard while Muslims were praying in there. He just didn't like me, and we'd often exchange nasty looks. I was protected while my Muslim bunkie was still there, but with him gone, he had it in for me for that reason. But it wasn't "their" room; it belonged to all of us. When I came to, we were both put into the hole separately until a determination could be made as to the instigator. When we were let out into the yard for an hour each day, there were only about 10 guys in the portion of the yard we were given. No more basketball, no more gym, no more being treated as even half human. Here I was once again back in a cell, this time with a gang banger from the Mexican gang named "18th Street," California's largest gang. He had tattoos everywhere, thereby claiming his alliance to the gang. We got along, and he came to respect me because I could do more push-ups than he could. Our co-existence was tolerable. To his credit, he did advise me to write to the officer in charge of solitary confinement to complain that my bunkie was a gang banger and thereby more dangerous to me than Mohammed (the man who hit me) who was classified for a high-security prison and not Fort Dix. Within days, they replied and released me back into the general population after spending three weeks there. My assailant was immediately sent to a high-security prison with other violent inmates.

I was no sooner released to the general population when my nephew drove up from Delaware to tell me that my oldest and last remaining brother, Arnie, had passed. For a full minute, I sat there in complete silence in disbelief. The last time I had seen Arnie was when he flew up from Florida to visit me in Valhalla. He cried so much, I had to ask him to stop because it was affecting me as much. That visit would remain with me forever as my last time with him. Just as when my father died all those decades before, I was not going to be able to say good-bye to Arnie either.

I had to appear before a judge in New Jersey regarding the charges against me for Mandy's checking account. There wasn't an easy system where they picked up a prisoner and delivered them to another location. It involved going to an interim prison first where you were processed and then waited for someone to move you. They took me to Philadelphia for processing where I remained for two weeks before driving me to the Hackensack, New Jersey, county jail.

At least in Hackensack I was closer to Debbie and my family, and they could visit me. Visits were limited to once a week, and when they did visit, we spoke on a phone through a glass partition for a few minutes while other women lined behind them to speak to their inmate. Like someone looking at puppies in a pet store window and all the dogs race to the glass for attention, hoping someone to take them home, I was a dog, and I desperately wanted to go home.

It was the middle of the winter, and the jail was so cold the inmates cut their socks and wore them over their arms because our uniforms were short-sleeved. After two weeks, my attorney finally visited me when Timi asked him why I was sitting in Hackensack and why we knew nothing about me or this case. He then responded and successfully made a deal, giving me no additional time behind bars. As soon as the case for Mandy's checking account was over, they returned me to Fort Dix. But I would have tolerated the cold in Hackensack knowing my girl was visiting me.

On the way to Fort Dix, the detective who was escorting me back remembered me from the ride down. He liked me very much, and he already knew my story. As soon as he saw that it was me that he was transporting, he announced it was lunchtime and he'd buy us both lunches. He asked what my favorite dish was, and when I said spaghetti aglio e olio, he pulled into his favorite Italian restaurant and ordered it for us both, confirming, "al dente, right?" I answered, "Yes, of course." When he returned, I was able to eat a genuine Italian meal for the first time in two years, albeit in the back seat of a police car. I don't think spaghetti aglio e olio ever tasted that good. Before reaching Fort Dix, I promised I would reach out to him when I was released and invite him and his wife to dinner at a restaurant that we both loved. I hadn't been treated like a human in years, and it came from a cop!

I was in the yard one day and started playing basketball. The game became a little intense, but nothing unusual for me. When we finished, I began walking back to my unit when I felt faint. I leaned against a fence and, luckily, was only feet away from the infirmary so I could walk that distance without collapsing. Inmates were not allowed to just walk in without a pass, but when the physician saw me, he immediately knew I was in distress.

The doctor called for an ambulance, and once I was put into the vehicle, the nurse who was riding in the back with me injected an IV needle into my arm while the ambulance was moving and proceeded to pass out herself. By the time she came to, my heart had already begun to beat normal again, and I regained consciousness. As she awakened, she looked up at me and asks, "How are YOU?" I respond, "Me? How are YOU?"

The prison had to be locked down for several hours until every guard was able to do a prisoner count after any vehicle, even an ambulance, came into the compound. My heartbeats had dropped to 30 beats a minute, so the decision was made to put a pacemaker in my chest.

Because of the pacemaker, I was required to be moved, again, to a federal prison with a medical facility, so I was sent to Devens, Massachusetts, an administrative facility, meaning it held inmates from different security classifications, i.e., white-collar criminals to mobsters and sex offenders. Here, too, I met other like-minded inmates who loved singing oldies, and together we formed a group, singing for the same occasions in church and the holiday events in the yard. The inmates loved us, my biggest fan being the famous underboss, John Franzese of the Columbo crime family the oldest inmate in Devens and still the dapper underboss with all his hair and teeth at the age of 95. Between playing chess, basketball, exercising in the gym, and singing, I was kept busy. In between, I emailed my kids and spoke with Debbie every day. I still didn't know if Debbie was going to wait for me; I had years to go.

I had arrived only days earlier in Devens when I heard someone say, "Low and behold, I can't believe my eyes!" With that, I turned to see for the first time in years my old friend and Jewish inmate Steve from Valhalla. As required by the federal prison system, we hadn't stayed in touch, and I was happy to see him.

While in the yard one day, an inmate came over to me after seeing Steve and I together and asked, "Is that your friend?"

Thinking nothing of his question, I merely answered, "Yeah. We know each other from Valhalla."

"Do you know what he's in for?" he asked.

"Yeah, tax evasion," I replied.

As if only happy to prove me wrong, he responded, "No, he isn't. He's a pedophile!"

Stunned, you could have knocked me over with a feather. It then made sense why he got 10 years and could not get bail. In Devens, I didn't see him often because we were in separate units and ate at different times, but we continued to go to Temple together on Friday nights, and I would occasionally see him at the gym. After a while, Steve knew that someone in my unit had to have told me the truth about him and asked me one day, "Have you heard anything about my situation?"

"Yes," I replied.

"I was set up," he explained. "I was online with a woman who told me she was 19, and she set up a date for us to meet. Just before we were to meet, she tells me she's really 13. I saw her photos, and she looked every day of 19, so I went. When I got there, she turned out to be a young detective, and I was arrested."

He hesitated, as if to get up the nerve, and then asked, "Do you think I'm a pedophile?"

After hearing his story, I felt somewhat sympathetic, but I knew he never should have gone. To argue over his past indiscretions came with a conversation I didn't care to have, so I simply answered, "No."

By now, I had use of email, but only to people on my approved list. We had no internet usage otherwise, and everything we wrote was likely read. That Wednesday night, I told Debbie what I heard about Steve and asked if she could look him up on the internet, and what she found shocked her as well.

Debbie had come to know Steve's wife Mary, but never regarded her as someone to stay in touch with after I was released. There was something about Mary that maddened Debbie when they planned a visit to Devens together to see us. Although they never discussed Steve's crime, Debbie had no reason to believe it was something other than tax evasion and didn't understand why Mary's family and friends were fiercely unsupportive of her continuing to have any relationship with him. She didn't treat him as an ex-husband either. She very much treated him as her husband, and the plan was to wait the 10 years for him. Why did her family and friends care so much how he reported his income if this woman loved him? Her oldest friends were walking away from her. Mary filed for divorce, but said she had to for her job. Not being her business, Debbie dropped the conversation.

Debbie sent me the information she uncovered, and I saw for the first time that child porn was found on his computer. He failed to mention *that* part to me. Do I really think he's a pedophile? Hell, yes! I'm no angel, but I don't sleep with children! Devens was not only a medical facility, but it was also known for housing pedophiles. They were safe there. If you violated one of them, you received a harsh punishment. Uncle Sam made sure they weren't hassled.

After Debbie's first trip together with Mary, Debbie kept her distance from her and only remained Facebook friends for some years. Mary continued to support Steve, but eventually fell in love with a woman and married her!

Two years had passed, and I had only seen Debbie twice. I'd have to wait to be released in November to see her again. I could see the light at the end of the tunnel, and Debbie is counting the days till my release. My calls to her left me confident the closer I got to November. I prayed it didn't snow. If she needed to travel four hours when the roads were dry, would she make it if it snowed? If she couldn't, I would be left there until the next day she did! Even if it's your release date, you're not allowed to just walk out.

Debbie rented a room minutes away from the prison the evening before her visit to make certain she'd be there to get me not a moment after 8:30 a.m. My heart raced at the thought of her running into my arms, no limitations on touching her, on kissing her. It was over two years without a human's touch.

Fifteen years had passed since we had been together. We were both different. I didn't know if she'd ever truly trust me or if she was able to get past our history. I didn't know if I'd wanted to revert to my old ways either, but I knew I promised her one thing: my fidelity. I also wanted to be worthy of her, for taking me in with no reservations and giving me a life, a beautiful life, to say the least, and the only way of achieving that goal was to reunite her with her family. She had just reunited with one sister over the illness of a niece, but there were problems, and I was willing to do whatever it took to make her happy after everything she did for me.

I often thought about our first kiss and how I approached it. She smiled at me, but I didn't know if she was flirting or just being nice. Saying good-bye that night in the parking lot, I made a childish bet with her, and if she lost, she'd have to walk to my car and kiss me good-bye through the car window. She was so certain she'd win and considering there was a door separating the two of us, she made the bet — and lost.

172

With all intentions of paying her full debt, with much trepidation she cautiously walked over, put her head through the open window, and gently placed her lips on mine. No tongue, just warm, soft, tender lips. I never forgot it.

But it was different, and I no longer had anything to offer her anymore. Nothing. And I had no Plan B.

From the moment I arrived all those years before, I had dreamed about that day; I just didn't know who would be on the other side of the gates. She was giving me another chance. In my heart, I didn't deserve it, but other than my daughter, she was the only other person I trusted. After two years of being caged and contemplating suicide, I took a leap of faith, swallowed the ounce of pride I had left, and mailed her a letter. I desperately needed her friendship. I needed her advice. I needed her.

That was six and a half years prior.

Walking that interminable, proverbial last mile was taking the whole experience in reverse. Each time I walked through a set of steel doors and heard the

173

loud, screeching clang locking me "out," my emotions heightened more than the previous set of steel doors. I was walking toward the light. I was going home; thank the good Lord, I was going home.

Chapter Eight

Switching Wardens

Arriving precisely at 8:30 a.m. as promised and not a moment later, Debbie traversed the snowy and icy parking lot into the prison. Walking to the front desk was a vastly different experience than any other time visiting me in any prison, beginning with the officer at the front desk initiating a conversation with her. He knew the recidivism rate. It's the last chance he has of giving it to you straight, a parting gift, a good-riddance — for now. With no one else in the room, he turned to Debbie to offer some unsolicited advice.

"He'll be back; they all come back," he cynically submitted.

"No, he's not!" Debbie quickly responded. "He's 72-years-old, and if he does something wrong, I'll personally drive him back to you, but he's not coming back as long as he is under my roof."

The guard, unwavering, answered smugly, "He'll be back unless you lock him in the basement."

Who do we blame? Why do more than 50 percent of those incarcerated return within three years? (43 percent within the first year of their release on a national average.) Who failed? Was it their mothers? Did they know enough about their son or daughter? Did they know their friends and their friends' parents? Did they know what they were up to? Were there signs that they turned a blind eye to? Were they too soft with them? Or was someone too hard?

I blamed it on my father for dying. Had he lived, I couldn't imagine what we would have accomplished together as a family — and still can't until this day. Gone over 60 years, I thought about him every day! I was 10 when he died. My mom did the best she could with what life dealt her. She came up short sometimes; her mind couldn't handle life without Dad, and soon she became disabled. I missed her raising me, cooking for me, telling me about girls when Dad was already gone, and I missed her telling me stories of my father at the dinner table. I missed so much! My father would have put an end to all the misbehaving from the start and I'd had never gotten so low. Without him, I didn't need to make anyone proud.

But is that an excuse? Once my father was gone, I had too much freedom and no woman to stop me, not my mother, not my aunts, not my house "mothers," and not my wives. But that was about to change. When I asked Debbie all those years ago in the Valhalla prison to be my girlfriend, she said, "Under one condition: I will treat you like a 12-year old," her voice elevating, "and you are punished for the rest of your life. Maybe, just maybe, I'll let you walk to Shop-Rite for your 75th birthday," she chided, jokingly, wagging her finger, almost popping out of her chair. I smiled; someone cared that much. I was all in. I knew I was going to be trading wardens when I left Devens, but I had no problem with it because I had her. I knew she ran a tight ship to achieve what she did, and I knew the toll it took on her to be able to purchase the home from her father's estate. Her first concern was always financial; I'd be the second, I thought, if I'm lucky. A religious and practicing Catholic, mostly conservative by nature, she'd never tolerate my old

177

ways. She was a strong, independent woman who didn't need me. We just happened to fall in love when she worked for me. I never committed to a long-term relationship when we met knowing I couldn't afford it anyway, but I knew I could trust her, and I remembered the chemistry, too. I absolutely remembered the chemistry.

I hadn't slept all night, so when the guard at my final stop before exiting the prison walls asked me to repeat my federal ID number, I went blank! Completely blank. I physically became weak. For 10 minutes, I waited for my body to regain normal blood flow to my brain before I was able to remember my number and repeat it to him. Had I not, I'd remain in their prison until the next day they asked!

At 72 years old, I was walking out alive. I didn't have the swagger I had; I didn't have the money I had, and I didn't have the youth I had! It was game over. Figure out another way. I was acutely aware that if it didn't work out with Debbie, I didn't have a back-up plan.

But I knew her, I knew her nature, and I fell in love with it before. I just never lived with her before. I never even dated her. What scared me the most was her anger. She was angry with her life and what her family was doing to her, she was angry with her father's caregivers, and she was angry with Richard for always lying to her. It was all unfair; she didn't deserve it. Lynn was sullen, Mandy was high, and I didn't want to live with an angry person now. My goal was to make her happy AND bring her family back together, which was a monumental task in itself. Whatever it was, we were going to be thrown together for at least six months while on home confinement.

As soon as I could recall my federal ID number, I was free to go. I'd be walked to the front desk. The front desk, like a normal person! Minutes later I walked into the lobby and there was my girl waiting for me — 10 feet away! As if in slow motion, she stood up and walked to me.

It wasn't anything akin to a Hollywood movie, where the woman runs into the arms of her newly released prisoner as the steel gates shut behind him. I was 72 and exhausted, so as my driver to the halfway house, she had to pick *me* up in the waiting room. Like a tired child, I fell into her embrace like a disjointed puppet. My feelings were somewhere between sleep deprivation and euphoria.

Wanting the same thing, we cut the hug short to exit the building as quickly as possible. As we held hands walking to the front door, the guard seized the opportunity to repeat his earlier piece of advice to Debbie.

"Remember what I told you," he insisted. "Lock him in the basement."

"He's not coming back!" Debbie repeated with confidence.

Walking out the door and stepping down the icy curb into the parking lot, I looked at Debbie and said, ironically "Well, that was a bumpy ride!" Just like that — as if I had gotten a traffic violation!

Let the new life begin!

I asked a guard one day what to expect when I reported to the halfway house. I already knew it was in Newark, New Jersey, and it was going to be in a tough neighborhood. The guard told me so assuredly, so nonchalantly, that all I needed to do was report there the same afternoon, and they'd set me up for going home. A piece of cake. I'd just report there, and I'd sleep in a normal bed by tonight — with an actual woman! I've been thinking of this night with her for years, and tonight's the night!

I handed Debbie the papers with my instructions for Newark before exiting the parking lot before advising her that I was on a clock to get there. If I didn't arrive within the time calculated to go the distance with a short lunchbreak, I could be punished. I hadn't had a mark against me in the 8 ½ years of time served, and I didn't want to begin then. I was looking to stay free, not get back in. Then Debbie told me that she still had her belongings at the hotel because she was running late getting to the prison.

Wearing clothing given to me by them, a jacket far too light for November in New England, no hat, scarf, or gloves and thin sneakers, the locals would

181

surely know where I was coming from. My other clothing had been mailed by the prison to my daughter's address. I was trying to fit in with society, but I felt like I was wearing the prison flag.

My head was whirling with everything going through my mind, the sleep deprivation making it more intense. I knew my chance to be alone behind closed doors with her could never be the encounter we had both fantasized about because of the time frame, but to be able to hold her and kiss her without armed guards watching us made me feel human again. Touching her was different than it was 14 years before. Our bodies were different; we were nearly 15 years older, but the hugs were the same. The kisses weren't as lustful, but love-ful. I didn't need to rip her clothes off; I needed her to hold me. I didn't need her to talk dirty to me; I needed her to kiss me without stopping.

On the way out of the hotel, Debbie handed me the cellphone she'd been speaking to me with over the last six years that was now mine! I had the power in my hands to speak to anyone I wanted! I called my kids, and when I phoned my old friend and employee,

Doug, to tell him I was out of hell, he cried. It was a joyous day!

Because of our detour to the hotel, we only had time to stop at Wendy's for lunch. Sitting together, two normal people, was as if "Scottie" had beamed me up to another planet. I didn't remember how this worked. *Were there waitresses? Do they deliver to the table? Do I leave a tip?* Like a kid in a candy store, I was in awe.

I telephoned the halfway house to advise them that we were stuck in traffic, and I was warned about arriving late. Already irritating people, and I hadn't even arrived yet. When we did arrive, I told Debbie to wait in the car and I'd return shortly.

It only took mere seconds before I realized that the guard in Devens had bullshitted me. I was not going anywhere for some time, and I hadn't even taken a suitcase with me; prisoners only walk out with the clothes on their backs. In disbelief, I had to tell Debbie I wasn't going home! As we drove away, she said emphatically, "I knew they weren't letting you go yet! I knew it!!"

I kept asking myself, "How did my homecoming dream go so terribly wrong?" How did it go from a real home to a real mess precipitously?" Somebody bullshitted me. That's how.

I had felt the warmth of her thighs hours ago, and I hadn't thought about much more since then. I had seen photos of the king-sized bed, and even if she was accustomed to sleeping alone, the bed was large enough to accommodate both of us. I didn't see how I'd ever let her sleep in another bed. Not most of the night, anyway.

I got another roommate alright, but nothing close to what I was expecting. Not only was I not sleeping with a woman that night, but I had to share a room with two other men — again! One, Black, and one, Palestinian.

Our room was set up with two sets of bunk beds, and, again, because of my age, I get a bottom bunk. I quickly tell the Palestinian guy that I'm Jewish, never knowing what to expect and never wanting to be surprised like another hit in the back of my head. We got along well, and the only thing we disagreed on was who owned Israel. Both roommates were repeat offenders.

There were four officers that ran the place, two of whom were women. Of course, my first question was "What the fuck am I doing here, and how soon can I get the fuck out?" They wouldn't lock down a time frame, but I was told one of the things required before getting approved to be released was a designated landline to the halfway house! Debbie needed to have a separate landline installed. I tell Debbie the situation, and she immediately makes an appointment with her phone company, but it's over a week away. On the day of the scheduled install, no one shows. Her phone call to them explained that there was no record of a new install, and a new appointment was made for another week or more away. Once the phone was installed, I notified the halfway house, only to be told that it wasn't the correct one. It needed to be installed by one of two companies specifically, neither of which was Debbie's carrier. A new account had to be established with a new carrier, taking weeks before an acceptable line was approved. Unfortunately, that still wasn't enough, and I'd have to serve more time there.

185

They had us on a short leash, a truly short leash, if we were permitted to leave the building. I signed up to go to Temple once a week and walked two miles to get there. In between, I was required to call from a "pay phone." It was already the age of cellphones, and between the two places, there was a total of one phone booth. And once I arrived at the Temple, I had to call the halfway house from the Temple's phone, and never from a cellphone because they couldn't track your whereabouts with it.

Other than that, I took the bus once a week to a drug seminar they offered just to get out. A bunch of guys and I got the bus conveniently on the corner that drove us directly to the drug class. It was the one time I didn't have to worry about calling because we were already watched.

When I received permission to leave for a doctor's appointment, I had to give them the details how I was getting there, and I always said by foot because that obviously took the longest time. Debbie met me once at a Subway for coffee, and another time we were able to sneak in a dinner at an Italian restaurant when I told them I was taking two buses to my appointment when truthfully Debbie was driving me.

My nickname became Mad Dog because I looked like a famous gangster, an ex-boxer, with that name. One day I met a young kid at the halfway house, a handsome white kid that I liked immediately. Respectful and friendly, we got along great. When I asked why he was there, I was a bit surprised when he said bank robbery. Bank robbery! That's ballsy. He didn't seem the type. Most of the kids I met were in for drugs. With noticeable trepidation, he kept asking about my nickname. Seeing the trepidation, I played with him, letting his mind go far with it was funny. I liked this kid a lot. I was convinced he was turning his life around with the help of his family.

It was Christmas already, and Debbie was allowed to visit. All the inmates and their visitors were packed into the auditorium for a few hours, and Debbie got to meet the bank robber. Not your typical "Bing Crosby" kind of Christmas. But Debbie wouldn't return for New Year's Day. She had been expecting me home for both holidays and was adamant about not spending another holiday in prison.

I'd be home soon enough. After a while, I was allowed a four-hour pass, and eventually I would be given an overnight pass. But that would take nearly three months!

On January 30, 2012, Timi picked me up, and I was released to six months home confinement with my new warden, Debbie. The difference was I was going to be sleeping with my warden, my mother, and my best friend! I don't know if it scared me or titillated me.

Debbie had just started a new job after receiving her master's degree, so she couldn't pick me up and have that Hollywood homecoming where I'd walk out the front gate. She had only been on the job for a couple of weeks, so she couldn't exactly explain why she needed the morning off. So, instead of that dramatic reunion with the steel doors banging behind me, she'd walk through her own front door and I'd be waiting for her. She told me where she hid the key, and Timi and I let ourselves into my new home.

It felt like no other home I've had. A stately brick home adorned with white balusters walking up to the front door screamed "Italians live here." Walking in, unlike Lynn's ultra-modern design, it was ancient Rome, Roman columns, big mirrors, paintings, and photos of Italy everywhere I looked — even the ceilings and doors. Her own Little Italy. Beautiful furniture and décor may have decorated every room, but there was a feeling of warmth, of welcoming. It felt like a real home that was lived in, not Lynn's showplace. Debbie left a note telling me she had a gift on the bed, a workout suit for the gym, my very first new piece of clothing in 8 ½ years.

After Timi left, I waited for Debbie to come home for lunch. While I waited, I inspected my new surroundings. Then I saw it: the Bengal cat, Nia. As beautiful as her photos, a mini leopard with her stunning coat and green eyes the size of saucers. I never liked cats, but I knew this was Debbie's baby. Stunningly beautiful, I could easily see why. As long as the cat didn't plunge at me or I wasn't allergic to it, we could live together harmoniously after all my years in lockup. A cat should have been my biggest problem!

At 12:45 p.m., Debbie walked through the door. Although excited to see me, it only took few minutes before she realized that she hadn't seen her cat. We frantically searched the house, but couldn't find Nia. Then Debbie realized what had happened: While I was saying good-bye to Timi as she was leaving the house, I held the glass screen door open to watch her pull away from the street, and the cat escaped the house behind my back. As an indoor cat with no front claws, she wasn't capable of surviving outdoors. I wasn't home with Debbie for 10 minutes, and I had already lost her cat!

After watching Debbie get hysterical for nearly the entire 30-minute lunchbreak, I noticed the cat near the front door and enticed her in with food. She was curious to be outside, but also afraid apparently. Debbie quickly ran back to work. That was on a Monday. On Tuesday, my second afternoon home, I turned a light switch on in the master bedroom and started a fire in the wall. In a matter of two days, I nearly lost the two most important things in her life! And this was the woman I was devoting myself to and promised to give a happy life, yet everything was going terribly wrong!

Debbie suffered from hot flashes, so even though it was the middle of winter, she slept in the cold, dark basement when I first arrived home. The bed wasn't big enough for the both of us to be comfortable all night, and she needed to sleep alone if she had work the following day. But before she retreated to the basement, she stayed with me in the king-sized bed until the weekend when she could stay the whole night. Kissing her, holding her ever so tightly, facing each other laying on our sides, she slowly slipped her knee between my legs, raising it until our bodies touched. It was the most intimate moment I had ever experienced. Feeling the warmth of her thigh, I knew that first night I was truly home — and I was staying until they took me out in a box!

But it wasn't so definitive for her! My first week home, I was more than anxious to talk to old friends, anyone. I knew I could never have any communications with Mandy if Debbie was in my life, and I wasn't going to violate that agreement. But everyone else was open game. My daughter Beth asked to visit with her mother, my ex, and her aunt. Beth's mother, Carol, was a hairdresser and said she'd cut my hair at the house, and I said yes before checking with Debbie. It was just a few days after I arrived at Debbie's and my first Friday night of freedom when they came to visit. Debbie was gracious about it with the knowledge I had no interest beyond the past we shared. But the tension became palpable after Carol cut my hair and grabbed my face with two hands like you would a child and kissed my lips. Debbie knew I did nothing to instigate it and said nothing while they were there. Carol could have done it at the door on her way in or out, but she did it in front of everyone. I tried to explain that it was just a welcome-home kiss, but Debbie wasn't buying it and was insulted. Debbie never felt threatened by her, but certainly disapproved of her behavior – especially when she snapped at Debbie for telling her how to clean up after my cut. Even though she didn't fault me, I still had to face her wrath. My daughter's mother wasn't welcome back. I would come to learn to ask first next time!

I quickly learned the differences between families and the way they spoke to each other. Debbie became loud when she was upset, and sometimes easily, but she wasn't nasty, mostly just loud. I was different with people, and I rarely raised my voice to anyone. But Debbie couldn't be changed nor did she want to. She was like a lioness sometimes, knew her own personality, and was very unapologetic. Her blessing and her curse as described by her priest. But I was a lamb in comparison; I handled people delicately. Debbie would sometimes get into a fierce conversation, some people might liken to a scolding – one you would not likely ever forget. I'm sure a great deal of it was cultural; there's no such thing as a quiet Italian woman. My second wife was Italian-American, but the only thing Mandy had in common with Debbie was they could both reach high audible levels at record speeds.

Having a new job *and* a new roommate was certainly not a walk in the park for Debbie. She hated her job, but accepted the position given that it was 2012 and the economy was in the depths of a recession. At least that job didn't demand more than normal work hours, was easy for her, caused no stress, and she was close enough to come home for lunch every day.

In the mornings, I'd make and pack her breakfast to bring to work. Once she returned home from work in the evenings, she cooked. If it was Italian food that night, we started with an antipasto made famous by her father, and served with warm Italian semolina bread. If the menu called for meat, she'd make it with mashed potatoes, a fresh vegetable in melted butter, and with a side of Italian semolina bread. It was a far cry from prison food. It was a far cry from anyone who ever cooked for me; Mandy only made reservations. Quickly, I found the 20 pounds I had lost.

After a couple of months, Debbie had confessed that the reason she backed away at times when I went to caress her was because she was embarrassed of her weight gain. We cut out the semolina bread and the mashed potatoes immediately. This was a woman who had a near perfect body when we were intimate all those years ago. But a long prison sentence and a hysterectomy later, we were different. Regardless, I couldn't get enough affection; I was insatiable. Debbie couldn't walk within a few feet of me without being grabbed. But the mornings were the best. I'd quietly hop into her bed, and because of her hot flashes, she'd only be wearing underwear. I'd press my chest against the warmth of her nearly naked body and rise to heaven. I began this ritual every morning for an hour before she had to wake up for work, and for four hours on weekends.

The landline Debbie had installed for the halfway house had a 20-ft. cord. If I was in the basement with her in bed, I had to leave the basement door open and run up the stairs if the phone rang. You never knew when the halfway house would call to check up on you — calling often in the middle of the night. If you didn't answer the phone, they'd have an officer at the door to pick you up and escort you back. You took the calls seriously. They'd immediately ask your federal ID number, and you needed to repeat it quickly. It was late one night when we were in her bed and the phone rang. By the time I was able to answer, the officer said, "What took you so long?" I replied, "I was having sex with my girl!" Stunned, he laughed and hung up. When I returned that week for a mandatory drug test and the officers saw me, I got a wink, a thumbs up, and a hand gesture indicating they knew exactly what I was doing, the guys' "attaboy." Everyone knew. I didn't care; I was 72 years old, but Debbie was mortified.

I was willing to do anything to make her happy. I began having telephone conversations with one of Debbie's sisters after her daughter had been diagnosed with Stage 4 breast cancer. It was a horrific situation, but the diagnosis brought the estranged sisters together after a 14-year separation. I became the buffer when any tension arose, and I became her defender. I was happy to have her back; it was the least I owed her. I would have work to do to get her Aunt Dee back, but I was up to the challenge.

One simple thing I was able to do was feed the cat, her beautiful, wild Nia. It didn't take but a few days for her to greet me each morning. The bedroom was on the opposite end of the house, but the moment I opened the door, she'd be at my feet looking to be fed. Her tail extending upwards to the sky like a proud peacock, I'd hold it until we reached her dishes, all the while practically singing "Good morning, Nia" repeatedly. It didn't take but a week before I loved her, too. She was sweet and not sneaky as I had imagined. Nia made us a family.

The longer I lived there, the more I loved it. When spring arrived, I was still attached to the phone and on home confinement, but Debbie purchased eight new arborvitaes, rented a truck, and brought them home where I planted them in the yard. I was planting my own roots. I enjoyed playing in the yard and graduated to the front as well, never being too far to hear the telephone. In the past, I had hired people for everything. The only thing I did was take out the garbage. Now, at 72, I was doing things I'd never done before and thoroughly enjoyed it. Debbie said I was like a disappointed 3-year-old when it rained and I couldn't go in the backyard. And not only did Debbie have everything for the house, but she also had back-ups. Some of her back-ups had back-ups. Extra hoses, all kinds of garden equipment, and enough extra furniture to fill another home, all of which was neatly stored away and organized. She knew where everything was. My favorite feature was the elevator she had installed when her mother became

197

handicapped. It was used as much as any of the doors. Overnight my life went from being locked up like an animal, to not knowing how I was going to store all my matzah on the main floor.

At dinner one night, I started to talk about the kid I met in Newark, the bank robber. I tell Debbie what a great kid he was and that he reached out to me on Facebook. Being the skeptic of anyone I knew, she listened and then ultimately told me I'm too trusting, I believe people too easily. She'd known me only with the worst of the crowds, but I didn't know this kid from anyone in my past. One night, while watching the news, I heard a report about a bank robbery in Newark. A young, white male called an Uber to take him to a few places. By the time the Uber driver took him to the third bank and realized what he was doing, he called the cops. He was arrested, and I saw it was the same kid I was so crazy about. After that, I stopped talking about what a nice kid he was.

On Friday nights after dinner, we'd make chocolate martinis, play music, and dance on the tiled kitchen floor. One night, as Debbie danced to Maroon 5's "Moves Like Jagger," — martini in hand, trying desperately to reach the high notes, her index fingers pointed toward the sky while moving them to the tune in an undulating motion, laughing — I knew I had fallen in love. Unable to hold myself back, I jumped out of my chair and grabbed her. I no longer feared the anger; I just had to learn how to handle it.

As it turned out, there was one thing neither Debbie nor I ever considered: I wasn't the one learning to deal with her anger issues, it was her having to deal with mine! If she raised her voice, I was easily offended, and the feeling of being back in prison came rushing through me. I felt crushed. Debbie always sensed it immediately and made every attempt to reassure me it was meaningless, but sometimes it took me days to recover. And probably like every Italian woman that ever walked the face of this earth, her temper could go off like a bomb. My most difficult adjustment was being in a normal relationship and having a normal disagreement. We rarely slept in separate beds the entire night, and as sympathetic as she was to my feelings, she couldn't realistically have a life never raising her voice. And If I didn't get enough affection, I pouted, not intentionally, but it was transparent, and I became a different person. The affection was like a drug I could not get enough of. Debbie said it was a full-time job in itself.

Just a few months after coming home, Debbie invited her cousin Cathy and her cat, Buster, to move into the basement after she lost her job. A clinical psychologist, she was interesting to be around when she was diagnosing Debbie's family. But my favorite tenant was Buster, officially making me a cat lover. He may not have had front claws, but he could throw a strong punch. When Buster heard us moving in the morning, he ran up the stairs and cried until I opened the door for him to join Nia for breakfast. Cathy became good company for me while Debbie was working. They would remain with us for nearly a year.

Once my home confinement was over, I started to look for some form of employment. Debbie didn't want me going back into sales and spending every night and weekends out of the house when she was home. I tried applying as a food delivery guy, but I'm sure they thought I was too old and didn't take me seriously. When the friend of Debbie's cousin Sammy asked me if I would drive her to work each day for a nominal fee, I agreed. Luckily, I was receiving a social security check each month and was, therefore, able to pay my own way. I just was not able to get ahead.

My first adventure out on my own in my new hometown was to the town barber, whom I affectionately called Johnny Haircuts. Friendly and a lover of Oldies, we hit it off immediately, and I was comfortable enough with him to tell him where I had been the last eight and a half years. Without trepidation, he and his wife treated me like any other customer they had been servicing for decades. I knew immediately I was in the right place, the right town, and since our first meeting, Johnny not only has never raised his price for me, he was happy to hang some of my old singing photos of me with Don & Juan and Freddie Scott.

A year to the day I moved in, Debbie went into surgery for breast cancer and, luckily, required only a lumpectomy and radiation.

It was the Jewish holiday Pesach, and we were invited to my daughter Beth's brother's home for the

Passover seder. Carol and her sister's family were going to be there. I wanted to see everyone; they were people I knew from my youth, and I wanted Debbie to go. Debbie agreed to go to please me and had gotten over the incident with Carol at the house stating, "everyone was tense." While I was driving her car, my phone rings. Being unfamiliar with the roads, Debbie answered for me and told the caller I was driving and would return his call another time. The caller was Mandy's son, my ex-stepson. When Debbie found out who it was, she became enraged.

The dinner was unpleasant for Debbie, to say the least. Not only was she in an environment with people she didn't want to be with, but the phone call on the way up made things that much worse. Prayer service at the house was nearly two hours before dinner was served, and Debbie sat with her back to me. No one asked about her cancer.

Over the next few weeks, Debbie and I fought over the people I wanted to maintain a relationship with. I wasn't going out with any of them; I was interested in merely talking to them to hear what they'd been up to over the last 8 ½ years. I wasn't going anywhere near Mandy, but when Mandy found out I was free after her son contacted me through Facebook, she started sending me messages stating, "We never had closure," desperately trying to get me to meet with her, reminding me "How in love we used to be." And because I had given my phone number to her son, she was able to get it. When I didn't answer her on Facebook, she sent Debbie messages as well. When neither one of us were answering, she tried texting me from her son's phone, signing "Love M." Her messages were erratic, which indicated to me that she was high when she sent them. High or low, I wasn't responding.

I had a choice years ago, and I chose Debbie, and never had I had any reservations. Unlike Mandy, she was there for me. Debbie was willing to overlook some things and wanted our relationship to work out for the mere fact that she had waited so long and didn't want to give up too easily. I had never lied to her, I vowed I wouldn't, and I was never going to go against her. She knew I had her back, I loved her, and because of that, she was more tolerant.

I eventually grew closer to Aunt Dee and her husband, Uncle Sal, and eventually we became friends. That New Year's Eve (the night before Aunt Dee's birthday), we invited them to dinner at a local Italian restaurant. I enjoyed every moment and had fun telling them Debbie's favorite jokes of mine. As we were walking out to leave, we passed a large bar area where a singer was performing some of the oldies. Slowing down, Debbie turned to me and asked, "Do you want to stay and listen for a while?" She knew I'd likely sing a tune with him before the night was over, but never in a million years did she expect my answer: "No, I want to go home. I miss the cat!" Debbie said she knew I truly had changed; I was finally content.

Cousin Cathy had just moved out of our basement when Debbie received a phone call from a mental hospital where her cousin Sammy, Cathy's brother, was a patient. Nine years her junior, Debbie and Sammy were close, regarding him more like a little brother, and over the years, Sammy moved into and out of her home five different times. A doctor was on the phone telling Debbie that Sammy wanted to return to living in her basement and was asking if Debbie would accept him back. Without hesitation, she agreed to pick him up from a mental institution and give up her bed in the basement. But there was a caveat: He'd be under her watch. No drugs and no bad friends.

Sammy moved into the basement, and the very next evening Nia was found dead in her bed. She had made it to 18 years old. When she couldn't make a jump she normally had no problem with, I knew something was changing, but I never expected her death to come so quickly.

Sammy was home on disability, so during the day we walked all over town together and he introduced me to all his friends and acquaintances. His favorite spot was the dog park. He could always pick up a girl there. You'd think after 50 years they would have heard enough of his cheesy lines, his bullshit, but they all enjoyed his company, both men and women. What a gift of gab! But Debbie didn't like most of his friends. One night after work Debbie and I took a walk together, and I suggested the park where I could introduce her to my new acquaintances. After speaking with them for an hour and getting to know them, she knew what they were about and didn't want me associating with them, knowing some of the girls were doing drugs and giving them to her cousin. It offended me that she dismissed them so quickly, and I felt she was being too righteous. It didn't matter how I felt, she didn't want me around most of these people, yelling, "she was known in this town with high regard and didn't want me associating with them. You are judged by the company you keep, and it will be a reflection on me!" I didn't appreciate it at the time. She sized them up and knew exactly who she was talking to. That's when I got to hear a lot about her mother, Betty, and what she taught her about the company you keep. Debbie wasn't having it.

Sammy was a real character, and I enjoyed his company especially when Debbie was at work. I needed to be around people other than my old crowd. Sammy and I watched "The Godfather" together, and after that, Sammy became so fascinated with the mob that he wanted every new person he met to believe he was connected to them, even introducing himself as a wise guy who was "put on the shelf" by the big boss. Who does that? I knew some actual members of the Cosa Nostra because I bunked with one of John Gotti's men, so I was familiar with how they spoke. They never mentioned the words Cosa Nostra. Yet, Sammy threw that name around as if he were the mob's public relations guy, which is the exact opposite of how a Mafia "made man" would act. When they asked him what crime family he was connected to, he would go blank. A real fucking gangster — not! He'd read up about Sammy Meatballs, and suddenly, he himself became Sammy Meatball's future son-in-law. The stories were out of a movie. He would tell Debbie crazy stories of being in a mob, how a leaf spoke to him about sexual abuse that occurred decades prior in the family, and how he reported the conversation he had with the leaf to the police. Debbie never asked if the leaf had a mouth. She'd dismiss his lunacy, feeling he wasn't harmful to anyone. She could do just so much for him. But Debbie and I both realized how bad he was getting when he refused to take his meds, spiraling downward, and then began abusing drugs and alcohol. Within a few months, we had to lock him out because of the people he was hanging out with and bringing home. He had broken his agreement with her, so out he went.

A few of my pre-Mandy friends returned to visit me when I first returned home, but life was different for everyone by then, and we never picked up where we left off. My old buddy, Hiram, an entertainer, was coming to NYC for an audition, close to our home, and we offered him to stay with us a few days. Debbie and I took him to the local café where the TV only played in Italian, ate cannoli, and drank cappuccinos. He'd comment in the morning of hearing our laughter in bed; he hadn't made his wife laugh like that in decades —and he was a comedian! He was welcome to return.

Soon thereafter Hiram needed to rent a place while looking for work in Manhattan, so he asked if we would rent out the basement to him for a few months. Knowing it was temporary, we accepted. Hiram was invited to eat with us nearly every dinner, so his stay to me was more like living with a roommate. But to Debbie, he was a tenant. She "could not live with two men," she'd complain. I alone "made her nuts." One night during dinner, the conversation quickly got heated over politics. I found his attitude offensive, and it got loud. After a while of hearing us go at it, Debbie threw us out of her kitchen and sent us to the basement. His stay became toxic for me, as I rarely ever raised my voice, but with him around, it was happening all the time. After decades, we parted.

In April 2013, 15 months after getting home, Debbie and I became engaged. No fanfare, no plans to get married, just engaged.

Debbie was turning 60 that year, and she had promised herself another horseback riding tour throughout Tuscany as she did for her 50th. A tour was booked for her alone that fall in Italy. I was still on probation. I couldn't just leave the state, and certainly not the country. If I didn't have their permission and something happened with me involved in any way, they'd return me to prison. I asked my parole officer about the possibility of getting a pass to visit Cape Cod, Massachusetts, and was advised to download the form. When Debbie realized the time involved to get possibly approved, it was too late, and suggested that I complete the form for Tuscany. I had nothing to lose. A one-page document was sent indicating Rome as the place of arrival and departure with the rest of the itinerary and, to our amazement, it got signed! Debbie immediately got me a passport. When I mentioned my trip to my parole office before leaving, she was stunned and accused me of lying to her. I explained exactly what happened and assured her I was not being deceitful and that I would not go but she'd have to have Debbie reimbursed for the ticket based on her signature. She simply replied that she'd get back to me. An hour later after speaking with the courts, she called and informed me I was permitted to go. She signed a one-page document without looking at it and was angry at me.

Debbie took it as a gift from heaven, a gift from her relatives for her 60th. I was just taking it with great pleasure and enthusiasm. I was following her anywhere!

Our first stop was Acquaviva, where we stayed in a tiny apartment on a pig farm deep in the mountains of Tuscany bordering Umbria. We were there to relax and see her friends, Maria and Angelo, the owners, before the riding began. Debbie vacationed at the farm several times and considered the owners friends after all the years of visiting. I finally got to meet Maria and her family I'd been hearing about for years and experience firsthand her hospitality and cooking, especially the prosciutto, worth the trip itself Debbie said. I was surprised and a little nervous to see how easily Debbie took the turns climbing the mountain to the farm with our rented 4-cylinder stick shift, driving as quickly as the Italians. When we arrived at the farm, no one was around, and when Debbie looked at the front door of the apartment she always rented, the key was in the door. There was a fire already roaring in the fireplace just waiting for us, thanks to Maria.

Neither Maria nor her husband spoke English, but with the little Italian Debbie knew, they were able to communicate to the point of making each other laugh. Debbie said Maria was the only person she was ever comfortable speaking Italian with. Maria understood her.

I fell in love with the family immediately, especially when Maria greeted us, yelling, "Debbie, Debbie, Debbie!" like a long lost relative. From there, the first spot to tour and visit was Cortona near the base of the mountain, the village made famous by the book and movie, "Under the Tuscan Sun."

After three nights, we reached our riding center in the stunning Val D'Elsa region of Tuscany. This particular riding tour was given only twice a year, so it was very surprising to Debbie when there are only two other women joining her, two female acquaintances from Colorado, although she was grateful that they hadn't canceled the tour with so few people. I was easily capable of keeping myself entertained with my iPad, a Wi-Fi connection, and an exercise room until they arrived back from riding each day. There was always someone around.

The drives through glorious vineyards such as San Felice and La Selva were as stunning as any oil painting except the beauty surrounds you, it bathes you. Driving down dirt roads lined with cypresses over 80' high, Debbie was in her glory. She said between the magnificence of the rides and the surprise of me being there "she hadn't dreamed that big!"

Days later, Debbie suffered a back injury from hours of trotting. Somehow, the only time she felt pain was when she laid down. So, finding it impossible to sleep, she was forced to give up nearly all of the rides that remained that week. Instead, we visited different villages and hamlets each day, went for spa treatments, and spent a day at the thermal baths in Rapolano Terme. Each evening we returned home before dinnertime to a feast at the center with the other riders.

Driving past Montalcino, known world-wide for its famous Brunello wine, we hit a village to stop and visit for lunch and a cappuccino. Walking up into the center of the village, we realized we came upon a festival, a *castagna* feast. The steep side streets were abuzz with activity, happy activity, people yelling from balcony to balcony, passing their famous chestnuts. The atmosphere of people screaming in Italian with such joy in their faces, got me overwhelmed with emotion. I had come so far from prison to here following Debbie to this place, her beloved Tuscany. Before we reached the top of the hill, I grabbed her in a stone alcove, pressed her against the building, kissed her, and told her I loved her. I had come from a halfway house, and at that moment, I was halfway to heaven.

In Rome, we had a small apartment just two blocks from the Pantheon on the third floor facing a piazza with a high-end restaurant that was always packed with motorcycles and cars double- and triple-parked. The bedroom was centrally located in the apartment, no windows, so noise was never a problem. We felt like real Romans, especially when we went food shopping. Handing the cashier my euros without speaking a word, they never knew I was not Roman.

In 2014, Debbie decided she could not live one more day with the soffits in her kitchen and began a major renovation on the house. Two separate contractors were hired. We couldn't afford to rent another home while under construction so we lived in it for 12 full months during the renovation. Debbie ended up being her own general contractor, which brought her closer to having two full-time jobs. Weekends and evenings were packed with shopping, researching, ordering, measuring, and painting all the wood ordered. By the time my 75th birthday came around, Debbie had had enough and surprised me with a suite at the Waldorf

Astoria Hotel in Manhattan for the night to celebrate my big birthday and get away from the construction.

The construction on the house was completed the week Debbie turned 62 and was retiring, so we planned to have a birthday/retirement party in our backyard. Fifty-five cousins came for Debbie's homemade ravioli while an Italian singer performed on the patio. But the surprise I had for Debbie was nothing she could ever have expected.

On Debbie's final day of work, I drove her to the office and told her that I needed the car for something. What she didn't know is that I planned to pick up a cousin, Junie, who she hadn't seen in over 20 years from the airport. They grew up in the same home as children, but were separated when her family moved away. Over the years, they had seen them so rarely that eventually there was no more contact at all. But after two decades, she had received a call from her cousin and felt a "sister" had returned to her. Joyous, Debbie planned that we would drive to her home in Florida, 1100 miles away, the day after her retirement party, so we could attend Junie's party that weekend — something we made up.

When I picked Debbie up from work that day for lunch, I was happily surprised when she told me she was not returning to work that day; she was retiring four hours early. Arriving back at the house, I told Debbie I had a surprise in the basement for her. Walking down the stairs, she thought it would be an item that was going to help her somehow with the party. An item. But when she was allowed to open her eyes, she had her long-lost cousin standing there right in front of her!

Screams and tears of joy could be heard down the block. I had never made anyone happier in my life! And it was exciting the following day when her sister and Aunt Dee arrived for the party and received an equal shock upon seeing Junie. The birthday/retirement party turned out to be an elegant affair, and someone even commented that it was like an outdoor wedding. Debbie gave the following speech:

"Over the last 44 years, I have had different careers. About 20 years were spent in outside sales dominated by men. One year after my father took ill, I was forced to find another job. It couldn't be an

office job because of my dad's needs. I walked into an interview one day and was hired for yet another outside sales position working evenings. A few weeks after I started, I met the very nice and very handsome owner. In a short period of time, I saw the difference between him and all the other salesman I had ever worked with. He was kind to everyone, the employees, and the customers! But he

was also kind to my dad. Over the four years I worked for him, I got to know him well, and we enjoyed each other's company. At the end of the fourth year, I saw trouble brewing and left his employment. We never spoke again. I heard of his troubles through a mutual friend and knowing his character - and his heart - it killed me. I spoke with my priest and lawyer, and they both advised to stay away. So, I did. But nearly five years later a letter arrived from him. This time I wouldn't turn my back ...

Obviously, we are talking about Preston. After living alone for three decades except for eight years with my dad, I was genuinely concerned about what it would be like living with him, especially considering he was much wilder than what I needed in my life! My faith has paid off; He has not only made my life fun for the first time, but he has given me my family, something money cannot buy. I want to thank you for the best birthday surprise I have ever received. To say you shocked me yesterday is an understatement. I not only got a present that lasts for seven days, but so did my family! I didn't dream this big! You are the love of my life, and my friends tell me my mom would approve. So, all thumbs up.

Just six weeks ago, I didn't think tonight was possible. I walked through a door and heard the worst words of my life: "Sit down, Aunt Debbie." But someone above pulled a rabbit out of the hat for my family, and I am so grateful to God tonight. I wanted to really celebrate this occasion; I still can't believe I am living the life I have always wanted - just being home with my guy. Ironically, my mom lost her life at 59 and mine started at 59. And tonight starts the beginning of the best chapter in my life and being with my family and friends.

You never know how life will change when you walk through a door. Here's to never hearing "Sit down, Aunt Debbie," and here's to La Famiglia!

For seven days, my girl was electrified with happiness. I gave Debbie what I promised: a man who was true to her — and I brought her family back!

In bed that night, holding her in my arms and looking into her eyes, I thanked her for my new life.

"Thank you for giving me one," she responded. God had surely answered both our prayers.

Three months later, we returned to Tuscany so that Debbie could begin writing her award-winning book, "My Love Affair With Italy."

Epilogue

We must all grow up and face life's challenges each passing day. What separates us as humans is how we react to these challenges and, ultimately, how we evolve.

If you begin to use hard drugs, your life turns to nothing less than a sea of sewage, as you are ultimately handing over your life to the devil himself. It may feel good for a while, but it's best described as skateboarding into hell. Choose your friends; don't have them choose you. Never be a follower because you may very well be following them right into the abyss.

Choose a spouse wisely. Looks are only skin deep and fade with time, sometimes very quickly. They should welcome your affection as much as you do theirs, as chances are you will be more likely to stay faithful to each other. Never choose a selfish person, for life will always revolve around them. If your friends and relatives tell you to slow down, take their advice.

If a friend needs help with something illegal, walk away because you are just as responsible. If you accept a person into your life knowing they are dishonest, don't expect better from them. There is no honor among thieves.

If you feel desperate and think there's no way out, never do anything that will lead to even greater troubles. Think first how it will affect your family before acting. No mother, no father, sister, brother, wife, or child wants to visit their loved one behind bars. It's a crime to the soul. Debbie is prayerful and believes not only were many of her issues resolved through God, but the Lord fulfilled many of her wishes to the point they far exceeded her dreams. She also believes in never going to the Lord empty-handed, meaning there's always someone out there that can use YOUR help.

One night while watching a detective movie in the communal room during one of my prison stays, an inmate said to me,

"Why do you always root for the cops?"

"Why not?" I replied.

He looked at me with a somewhat surprised look and said, "They put you here!"

I hesitated before replying, "No they didn't; I put myself here. The cops just did their job."

Annoyed with my response, he walked away in a huff.

That explains the difference between most of the prisoners I met and me. I always said I didn't belong in prison, meaning, although I did deserve to do time for my crime, I knew why I was behind bars. It was all my doing.

Everything we do is based on the choices WE make. It's not your parents for dying, your past relationships, your spouse or your kids, your job, the economy, an argument, or your age. You and only you are responsible for every decision and every choice you make.

What I am most proud of is walking out of prison a better man than when I walked in, which I attribute to remembering the family I knew as a child, however short. I appreciate life, liberty, and the American way far more.

Our life here is temporary; it's all about time. How we use this time matters in the end. I was lucky to have someone who had loved me enough, someone I respected, to not only wait for me, but who made it easier for me to take the right path. Not only do I love my freedom, but I love the fact that I don't have to look over my shoulder anymore. NO ONE is coming to arrest me — ever again!

Thank you for taking the time to share my story with you! If my story has touched you in any way, **please leave your kind review on Amazon.com or Barnes and Noble** and check out more of our story and see the photos by visiting:

www.DebbieMancuso.com

Or

Facebook.com/MyLoveAffairWithItaly

Or

Send us an email: Dmancuso310@gmail.com

Blessings!

Made in the USA
Middletown, DE
19 May 2021

39351570R00144